Table of Contents

Preface

Over the years, I've been fortunate to have the opportunity to help many people. My work as a consultant has been very rewarding, with results that often stretched beyond the business world. It's felt amazing to see my method applied to improve marriages, family life, and friendships.

I often wondered if there was a way to reach a larger audience, but authoring a book was always out of the question in my mind. I barely finished high school, and have always struggled with learning disabilities. If you told me 5 years ago today that I'd be writing the foreword and acknowledgement for my second business book, I would have laughed in your face.

Eventually, the desire to help others would overcome my insecurities. I put my ego aside and made the move. But that never would have been possible without help; I've been supported by some very smart, talented, and caring individuals in my life, and I'd like to thank those people here.

First, to the love of my life, Galit. Thank you for the love, support, and hard work you've given me through all of our years of marriage. With you, my life is complete.

Next, to my kids. Gaya, Ely, and Liron, it wasn't until I became your father that I truly understood myself. You've shown me what's truly important in this world. Each of you are special in your own way, and I know that you'll keep making me proud.

To my mother and father, you've made me who I am today. Dad, you've always seen the world through a very special lens, and I am so thankful that you passed that perspective down to me.

Mom, you gave me your heart, love, and charisma. This book was inspired by the desire to help others that you bred into me. You taught me to always be kind, and that you don't become a good person only when it suits you.

Tal, my brother, you're one of the best salesmen I know. You're blessed with natural ability, and I'm blessed with a big brother who's willing to share his gift. Every conversation with you teaches me a valuable lesson, whether you realize it or not.

Osher, you are my sister and my life coach. You're an incredibly special woman with perspective and sensitivity I could only dream of. Every time we talk, you inspire me to explore another new path in life.

Gali Peles, thank you for everything you taught me while we built our first web design company together. Without you, I would have never known my full potential.

David Polsky, you're one of the smartest people I know. I couldn't have mustered up the courage to pitch to big companies without your support. You taught me how to swim with the big fish. Thank you; I look forward to many more years of business and friendship.

Oshri and Eli, you redefined dedication in my eyes, and showed me the true value of hard work. Thank you both.

Gal Agassi, you're a true marketing guru. I thought I was a marketing master when we first met, but working with you has taught me how far I have to go. I look forward to learning even more from you in the future.

Koby, you inspire me every day with your fire and focus. No matter how difficult, you always accomplish your mission. You've taught me more than you know.

Jeff, I'm a self-proclaimed "numbers guy," but you wear the crown. I've never seen somebody break a real-world business scenario down into data like you; I've watched you assess the viability of a business in 10 minutes flat. Thank you for showing me something new every day.

Brandon Rea, I had the opportunity to write this book alongside experienced writers with established names, but I chose you. Thank you for the hard work: I know no one could have done a better job.

Lastly, I'd like to thank the thousands of prospects, customers, and vendors I've worked with over the years, and those I continue to work with today. Without you, my evolution would have stopped long ago.

Introduction

My name is Lior Izik. I've been in business since I was 10 years old, buying bagels on the street and selling them to bankers two doors down for double the price. Since then, I've come a long way, and experienced a lot of what the business world has to offer. I've worked as a lifeguard, gardener, dishwasher, garbage collector, masseuse, acupuncturist, marketer, web developer, security expert; the list goes on.

My experiences have not all been good. I'm no stranger to spectacular failure. I've created many companies in my career, some of which hemorrhaged money and closed after being in business for only a few months.

Though they hurt and embarrassed me at the time, these experiences made me the man I am today. Some of the most important lessons I've ever learned came out of catastrophe. Without my failures, I would never have developed the philosophy that turned a street-side bagel broker into a successful entrepreneur.

I learned from my mistakes, and fought for a winning record in the business world. Much of this occurred on the internet; my web design, development, marketing, and security companies did great despite being surrounded by strong competition. Some of my ventures were sold to bigger companies, and others are still making me money today.

It wasn't long after I sold my first business that I began my consulting career. I always wanted to help people, and was excited to test my philosophy in different industries. To my delight, it passed; real estate agents, home services companies, call centers and law firms all benefitted from the lessons I had learned. This changed the way I functioned in the business world; rather than creating my own companies from scratch, I began to merge into existing businesses as a partner and full-time consultant. Today, I am associated with a number of successful businesses, and am happy to have been given the opportunity to help them grow.

Why I Wrote This Book

I believe in completely transparent business practices, so I'd like to take a moment to explain my motives.

I wrote this book because I want to help people. My mother raised a boy with a lot of empathy; I'm very sensitive to people's "pain points," and have found few sources of pain greater than the struggles of small business owners.

Though my ultimate goal is to become a man who gives unconditionally, there's still a selfish motivation behind this book. When you help someone, you feel good - they say "giving is the greatest gift of all" for a reason. I got a buzz every time my consultations helped someone boost their bottom line, and I sometimes wondered how it would feel to help thousands of entrepreneurs at once. Writing this book would make that possible. You can call me an endorphin junkie if you like, but there's plenty of good to be had in selfish giving.

I've filled this book with the information I wish I had when I first started out. The business world isn't easy, and quality advice is hard to come by. Generally speaking, business owners have three options when trying to learn the ropes of entrepreneurship:

1. You study business in university. This theoretical approach has value, but I don't think it's the best way to prepare yourself for the rigours of the real world. Curriculum material can sometimes be more impressive than it is practical. Business graduates leave their Alma mater without any idea of where to begin, or any hands-on experience to speak of.

2. You try modeling your business in the image of a big company. It may seem like a smart move to reverse-engineer the success of industry giants, but it won't help you. A small business cannot operate like a big enterprise. These companies are playing in an entirely different league, with the money and manpower to make their strategies work.

3. Trial and error. This is probably the most valuable approach, but it's dangerous. Trial and error will teach you the dos and don'ts of your industry, but a single misstep can be all it takes to bring you down. This option takes time, too - you don't become a seasoned veteran overnight.

I want to give you all the benefits of the trial and error approach, only faster and without any of the risk. This book isn't full of textbook theory, and it doesn't waste time with Fortune-500-level advice; I've distilled 22 years of small business ownership experience into 19 fluff-free lessons that will change the way you see entrepreneurship. I've tried and erred, so you don't have to.

I want your business to evolve - that is my end-game goal. I've designed these chapters to equip you with the knowledge and resources you need to lock your company in a constant state of evolution.

Evolution is formless, dynamic, part of a feedback loop whose outcome is never final. This is exactly how your business process should look if you want to contend with the curveballs that life will throw at you. This is why rigid textbook curriculums just won't work; as Bruce Lee famously said:

"You must be shapeless, formless, like water. When you pour water in a cup, it becomes the cup. When you pour water in a bottle, it becomes the bottle. When you pour water in a teapot, it becomes the teapot. Water can drip and it can crash. Become like water, my friend."

I designed my philosophy to be like water. I've combined hard-fought life lessons with a unique method of objective analysis to construct a problem-solving philosophy that can thrive in any business environment. These lessons can work for a one-man show, or an established small business. Rather than prescribing a strict set of actions, I help you understand the thought process behind my most successful moves. Once you've done that, you'll be able to adapt to any situation. You'll tap into your own creativity, and innovative ways to work around obstacles. You'll start setting and achieving goals you never thought possible. Your ability to make money, keep money, manage employees, and retain clients will improve.

How To Use This Book

If you've never consulted with me or taken any of my courses, skip chapters 1-11. Read from chapter 12 onward, and start implementing these strategies right away. Start back at the beginning once you've finished. This is the same approach I use with new clients. They won't fully absorb my lessons until they know they can trust the source, so I lead with the quick, high-yield solutions. Once they've had some success with my method, I explain the deeper concepts.

Finally, a word on the format. In each chapter, a common business problem is identified, a specific solution is offered, and the rationale behind the move is discussed. Each chapter contains actionable advice that is easy to implement, and ends with a quick "elevator pitch" of the idea to reinforce the bottom-line message. You can use "The Bottom Line" at the end of each chapter like the abstract of a paper; take a quick glance to familiarize yourself with the core idea, then circle back to read from the beginning.

Redeeming Your Free Outsourcing Course: How to Work With Freelancers

The content put forth in this book interfaces with an online course I created in 2015 to help employers outsource work, which I'm now making available to readers for free. This course distills over 15 years of outsourcing experience into 10 fluff-free lessons that give small business owners the knowledge they need to make the most of this cost-effective market. The video, audio, and textbook components make for an easy learning experience, and the entire course can be completed in about two hours. Using the best practices I describe, your small business will be able to expand its service offerings and tackle new challenges without worrying about in-house hiring, training, and expenses.

You can look over the course rubric and curriculum in full at http://employer.rapidbusinesslessons.com. Once you're there, click "Get Started" and enter coupon code "employer-dream" to redeem your free membership. You'll also be given access to unlimited copies of our freelancer course, which is meant to be distributed to all outsourcing hires to ensure everyone is working from the same playbook.

Chapter 1:
Aim Before You Shoot

If you want to achieve anything in life, you need to identify your target, and go after it with single-minded focus. You must prepare and pursue clear objectives with the kind of urgency and organization that you'd expect from an Emergency Response Team (ERT).

When an ERT responds to a threat at an airport, you'd better not block their path. They will run through old vacationers and little kids caught in their way without a second thought. They focus only on locating their target and neutralizing the threat. In their minds, they see only their objective – everything else is just noise.

Aim Before You Shoot

You need to pick a target before you can hit a bullseye.

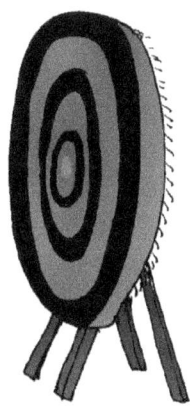

Biplov '16

The Entrepreneurial Evolution

That's exactly how you should handle your business. Now, obviously I'm not telling you to push past old folks in the grocery store to get your family dinner on the plate an hour early, or to steer your car through a school crosswalk to get to your office on time. What I'm saying is that you must identify a target, then block out any distractions in pursuit of this business goal. It's one of the most important things you'll ever do for your career. Your business won't be successful until you've defined success.

Setting and meeting goals is something that most people are taught in grade school, but it gets forgotten faster than long division. Lucky for me, the importance of goal-setting has been hammered into my head all my life; my experience with the military, the business world, and the martial arts taught me how small goals and incremental improvements add up over time.

Unfortunately, many people don't bother setting goals, even for massive undertakings, like raising a family or growing a business. When asked how they raise their kids, they'll tell me: "I do the best I can!" This is an answer I often get from very intelligent people, and it baffles me every time I hear it. How do you expect to get anywhere without an idea of where you're going?

Planning is vital; even when you're going to bathroom, there needs to be some kind of plan in place. You'll walk in, do your business, flush, wash and dry your hands, then walk out – mission accomplished. Shouldn't you put at least as much effort into raising your family and growing your business as you do into your bathroom breaks? These are the most important things in your life, and they deserve more than a laissez-faire future. Anybody whose washroom plan is to do the "best they can" is probably about to miss the bowl, and the same goes for families and businesses that don't think about their end-game approach.

Some people fail to set goals because they feel as though life is too unpredictable. Granted, building a business and raising a family is extremely tough, and there is really no clear road map, but that shouldn't stop you. Your plan doesn't need to be perfect, it just needs to point you in the right direction.

Deciding on the right plan for your family is highly personal. You need to weigh your personal values and build from there. For me, honour, respect, and persistence are key. I've decided that my children will involve themselves in sports daily. They will never lie to their family, or quit something they've started. My role is defined in the plan, too; I will feed them more healthy food than junk, tell them "yes" more than "no," and do everything in my power to build on their strengths. These things are important to me.

I can't make your plan for you, but I can say for sure that your family must be involved in the planning process. It seems so obvious to me now, but it took me years to figure out. How can you expect your family to participate in a plan they don't know about, or work towards goals that mean nothing to them? To not involve your family in the plan-making process is to railroad their lives, and hundreds of books have been published about how unhealthy that can be. If you want your family to work together, every member's voice must be heard during the planning stage.

I built my plan with my family, and we all agree that we're on the right path. We share the same goals, and life is good as we work towards our target together. When my cell phone rings with an important business call, I never have to scream for my kids to shut up. They turn mute, because they know that business calls like these get us closer to the things we want. My family is a team, like the Emergency Response Team surging through the airport. We plan our attack together, and every member knows their role. Before I began writing this book, my wife and kids were briefed, shown the target, and made to understand what's at stake. They were a big part of the process, and they've read over every word.

Planning in business must be approached in the same way. Family and business are mutually dependent - you work to support your family, but you won't get any work done without your family's support. You can't plan for one without the other.

Like many families, many businesses have no goals beyond some abstract idea of "success." Business owners around the world are emptying their clips without a target in sight, and it's costing them time, money, and enjoyment.

I met a company owner over dinner once, and between bites of asparagus shoots and steak he told me how his business was killing him. He was working himself way too hard, and it was wearing him down.

I couldn't believe what I was hearing, not because I didn't think he was working hard, but because I couldn't understand why he would be. I knew this man as someone who wanted nothing more than to be on a hammock, swinging between palm trees and staring at the shore. What was stopping him? He already owned a few properties, and had a very healthy savings account. At this point, no amount of hard work was going to get him into that hammock any faster. He was battling it out at the office for no reason, swinging punches with his eyes closed when the fight had already been won.

All this man needed to do was have a plan in place, and his both life and outlook would change for the better.

I'm talking to him, and to you when I say this: stop and create a plan right now. First, take time to decide on what you really want in life. It's a big question, and it deserves a lot of thought. Once you've decided on something, imagine yourself being one step beyond your goal, and ask yourself again if you would be fulfilled. If you think something might be missing, add more to your end-game goal, until you see yourself being truly happy.

Once you have a goal in mind, you can start to formulate a plan. Don't worry about specific details at this stage - this is meant to be a big-picture plan that simply points you in the right direction. The plan must suit your life and your capabilities, and your family must be involved in its creation; if you're married with 2 kids, you can't plan to work for 16 hours every day. Once the end-game target is set, you can break your plan into smaller goals, and start filling in the details involved in every step.

The Bottom Line

The bottom line is that your business will go nowhere if you don't have an end-game in mind. You won't be successful until you've defined success; if you don't aim before you shoot, you're just wasting bullets.

Decide what you really want in life, and create a big-picture plan to achieve it.

Chapter 2: Emptying Your Cup

As a child, I wanted a bicycle more than anything. When my parents agreed to buy me one, I was over the moon, though I knew I'd have to wait; I had a little experience peddling bagels by then, and it gave me enough of a business mind to realize a bicycle would take some time for my parents to afford.

Emptying Your Cup

What if you could get this excited about your job?

Biplov'16

The Entrepreneurial Evolution

For almost two years without fail, I would rush outside in the morning to see if there was a bike leaning against the house, waiting to be discovered.

I often think about the first morning I laid eyes on it. I didn't know it at the time, but I was setting the stage for one of the most important business lessons I would ever learn. I clambered out of bed and made my way around the house as usual, though this morning was anything but.

The bicycle I had dreamed about for more than seven hundred nights had suddenly appeared. A flood of joy and excitement washed over me, and I thanked my parents with tears in my eyes. The emotional payload hit home, and it left a massive impression.

Today, I can relive the entire experience in vivid detail. I can see my bike's shiny blue frame, skinny wheels, and long spokes. I remember my first ride, wrenching the handlebars left and right to find my balance, and the thrilling breeze I felt when I pedaled hard enough.

For some reason, I cared more for that bicycle than anything I've bought in the thirty-five years of spending since. I can't think of any other consumer experience quite like it.

Why can't I point to a single purchase that has had this same effect? After all, it was only a bike. I'm an adult with a magic Credit Card; online stores never close, and with a long line of credit to climb, I can consume almost anything I want with a few easy clicks. I've bought expensive technology, cars, houses, and entire businesses that made zero impact on me by comparison.

I needed to know why this one event was so significant when so many others just flitted by. My search lasted many years, but looking back, I'm glad I asked these questions, because the answers helped my family and business life in a big way. In fact, they helped form one of the cornerstones of my entire business philosophy.

The Empty Cup

A metaphor found in the wisdom of Kabbalah (www.kabbalah.info) helped me understand why the blue bicycle meant so much to me:

In the wisdom of Kabbalah, our enjoyment of all things is equated to the act of filling a cup. Simply put, the amount of enjoyment or satisfaction you derive from something depends on the "fullness" of your "cup" at any given moment. Filling your cup is the best feeling you can get, so the emptier it is, the more enjoyment you are able to receive.

However, the cup is not bottomless, and it can overflow. As the cup fills, your enjoyment level tapers off until it reaches a maximum amount. Once filled, you are fulfilled, and anything extra being added will spill out and go to waste. You'll no longer derive happiness from whatever experience was filling your cup, until eventually you wish it would stop.

The cup empties over time. Once you understand this, you can use it to your advantage. I reference this metaphor often, and want to be sure it's clear - let me give you an example:

Last week, I got a call from my wife around 9:00 a.m. She had just gotten home from the grocery store, and was planning to make my favourite dish for dinner. I was happy to hear it, but not overly excited; I had just finished breakfast, and didn't have much of an appetite. My cup was quite full.

I decided to skip lunch to honour the amazing dinner my wife prepared, and felt my cup starting to empty around noon.

By 4:00 p.m., my cup was well below half-full. Images of crispy baked potato skins and sour cream crept into my mind while I sat across from clients.

I finished my last meeting around 7:00 p.m. and hurried home. By this point, my cup (and my stomach) was nearly empty. The phantom smells of fresh dill and fish baking in the oven haunted me as I fought through traffic.

By the time I got to the dinner table, I was salivating. Every sense was piqued as my wife set my plate down in front of me.

I speared an oversized hunk of fish and potato onto my fork, and began to fill my empty cup. My first bite was pure bliss. It was the kind of feeling you only get with the first drop, and I took a moment to savour it. My wife laughed at the look on my face. The second bite was delicious. I tucked in to a perfect meal.

Though I knew objectively that every bite was amazing, I felt my enjoyment level drop as I ate. I slowed on my second helping. Eventually, I was stuffed, and a little uncomfortable. Another forkful would have hurt.

In that moment, my cup couldn't hold another drop, but it would empty in time. If I wanted the meal to be amazing again, I would just have to wait. I was craving my dream dinner again two days later.

This metaphor of the empty cup can be applied universally. Anything can feel priceless when it's gone, and worthless when it's abundant, even love

Think back to the blue bicycle - after waiting two years for my chance to ride, my cup was bone-dry. Anticipation had drained it of every last drop. When I saw my bike at long last, my cup was filled in a flood of joy and gratitude. It was a tsunami wave of excitement that hit me hard enough to leave a mark thirty-five years later.

Seeing my first bike was a feeling I could never replicate as an adult, because my cup was always brimming. My little drips of enjoyment weren't satisfying because I never let my cup empty. I just kept on consuming, wasting thousands on purchases I thought I needed to be fulfilled, when all I had to do was start limiting myself. It's so obvious to me now; you can't quench your thirst if you don't let it build.

Many people make the mistake of keeping their cups full at all times in our current consumer culture. It is an easy trap to fall into because it feels so natural to consume in a world filled with sales pitches and product placement. We associate consumerism with success, power, and enjoyment, but is that the reality?

It may sound better to keep a full cup and want for nothing, but it's not. The average household income has shot up in the past 30 years, but, despite all of this new luxury, people are taking record-high amounts of antidepressants. We want for nothing, but in doing so, we deprive ourselves of profound happiness and gratitude.

Human beings have a natural reward system in place that you can take advantage of through discipline. There is absolutely a positive correlation between anticipation and enjoyment; once you recognize that, you can enhance any experience you choose, whether it be a meal, a relationship, or a business task. If I want to really savour something, I just have to empty my cup a little before I go to the well. By limiting what you consume, you can control the amount of enjoyment that you derive from any experience.

The No-Business Diet

After a career as a competitive martial artist, I've exhausted my patience for most "diets." That isn't to say I am against healthy eating, but limiting myself to the same plate of steamed greens and white fish to make weight for fights got very stale.

Thankfully, the No-Business Diet has nothing to do with food. Rather, it's a mental technique that builds off of the Empty Cup idea. If you know how to empty your cup to increase your enjoyment of a thing, you can use the same technique to increase your productivity and trigger inspiration the next time you fall into a rut at work.

By now, you already know that walking around with a full cup is a big problem. The more you indulge in the same thing, whether it be work, food, games, or company, the more your enjoyment of that thing declines.

When this happens at work, your business suffers. Without enjoyment, you lose the energy you need to work effectively. How are you supposed to smile at sales meetings, project your voice, and show interest in your client without any passion? You end up working much harder for results that are much less rewarding. It's a terrible waste of valuable time and effort.

When you're an employee, there isn't much you can do about working with an overfilled cup. You have a mortgage to pay, a family to feed, and a retirement to fund, which means you're going into the office whether you like it or not. You won't be as motivated or productive as you were on your first day there, but that's okay; your paycheck is coming.

When you're self-employed, things change. A dip in productivity is no longer acceptable. There are no steady paychecks, and sales don't make themselves. You need to know how to empty the brimming cup that's holding you back.

Rather than banging your head against a wall at work, try the No-Business Diet. This diet restricts business thoughts in the way you would normally cut out certain foods. Rather than limiting what you consume to empty your cup, you limit your work.

Take a few days off, and disconnect yourself completely from the office - no business allowed. Make it known among your clients and staff that you will not be checking emails, but that they can call you if something really urgent pops up.

You won't lose money or miss sales opportunities by doing this. If you're a big company owner, you can delegate your duties for a few days. If you own a smaller company or have no employees, then email your clients and let them know that you're taking a short vacation. In my experience, clients who are made to wait a bit will want your business more than ever - their cups empty, too.

Just like any other meal plan, the key to success with the No-Business Diet is to deprive yourself of the thing you are craving the most. When I dieted for my fights, I wanted nothing more than a big pizza and a pint of ice cream, but indulging in either would have prevented me from making weight. Similarly, if you want results with your business, your diet must be strict. You'll crave work updates, but don't allow yourself any. This means no texts, emails, or other work engagements during your break. Distract yourself when business thoughts begin to creep into your head. The point isn't just to be absent from work, it's to stop working entirely until your cup has emptied.

Have you ever noticed how many people seem to come up with their best business ideas while they're on vacation? You might be one of them. After a few days of lounging poolside guzzling pina coladas, you start to think about work again. You couldn't get away fast enough before; now, you miss the action, the chase, and the feeling you get when you close a big deal. This excited energy is where great ideas are born, and it's the richest source of productivity.

Anytime you take a dedicated break from your business, you'll come back stronger. Finally able to satisfy the work cravings that had been eating away at you, you'll attack your projects like I attacked a box of pizza after every fight. You'll make up for the days you missed, and then some.

The No-Business Diet is as simple as taking dedicated time away from work; you don't have to take a beach vacation, and you don't even need to take a full three days off. You just need a weekend, wherever those two days may fall. This should be a normal weekly thing.

Finding break time is easier said than done. People think that self-employment means more free time, but it can make work tough to escape. I went more than two decades without a single day off. There was always some urgent task keeping my attention. It wasn't until I failed to recognize pictures of my baby daughter that I realized I'd been consumed. Even then, I had trouble justifying time off. How could I afford a break? My business goals had not yet been achieved.

When I learned about the theory of the Empty Cup, I realized I could have everything I wanted. I could put my best effort into my business without neglecting my family life. Knowing I would come back stronger, taking time to myself felt like an investment in my business. It was win-win.

Some No-Business diets have to be more hardcore than others. Think of the difference between a healthy eating plan and a crash diet or cleanse. I needed a serious decompression period after my twenty-plus year grind.

For hardcore diets, the best approach is to combine your normal weekend with plans to be out of the office on Friday and Monday. This gives you four days to empty your cup and jumpstart your productivity, and it only costs you two days outside of your normal work week.

If you're a workaholic, I promise you'll have incredible results. You get to enjoy four days to yourself, and you'll attack your three days in the office with an overflow of creative energy. It works for me; my family is closer than ever, and my businesses are booming.

You don't have to step away from your company entirely to get the productivity-enhancing results of the No-Business Diet. You can use the same approach on a smaller scale, giving yourself a break from specific tasks that have been wearing you down. If you've hit a wall, just step away from that particular project for a week. Assign someone else to cover you so that any clients involved don't feel neglected. Use your energy on another project in the meantime. When you return to your task with an empty cup, you'll make great headway.

I've gotten a lot of use out of this technique while managing projects as an IT consultant. In the past, I often dealt with teams of developers who would hit a wall, then burn weeks trying to solve the specific problem they were having. I'd be paying a competitive hourly rate for almost no results. Eventually, I began putting the developers on a No-Business diet, telling them to set the problem aside for one week while they completed other tasks. I would usually get an email a few days later from a team member reporting that they'd found a solution. All it took was some fresh eyes, and an empty cup.

As I mentioned previously, the principles of the No-Business Diet, and of emptying your cup in general, can be applied almost anywhere. I have seen marriages saved by couples who understood that their cups must be emptied. They say that "absence makes the heart grow fonder," and that is really the crux of the diet being proposed here. If your marriage has stagnated and divorce is being discussed, take a break for 1-2 weeks. Disconnect completely from your partner. You don't have to physically get away - both partners can simply agree not to talk to one another for a predetermined amount of time. Socially switching off in this way may sound cold, but you'll find that it plays out more like a game. If you have children in the house, tell them that the two of you have made a bet on who would crack first so that they aren't affected by this new dynamic. A few days into this experiment, you will probably start to feel the urge to talk to reconnect with your partner. These stirrings in your heart are a good sign for your relationship, but don't give in yet! If you agreed to 2 weeks, stick to the plan. It might seem excessive, but it is nothing compared to a divorce. Allow your cup to empty, and within 1-2 weeks, the passion will either be reignited, or pronounced dead. Whatever the final outcome, you will know you've made the right choice.

The Bottom Line

The bottom line is that knowing how and when to empty your cup will enhance your life, and seriously improve your business. By limiting what you consume and adopting the No-Business Diet as needed, you can become more productive, rediscover your inspiration, and make more Blue Bicycle memories. Think hard about this lesson as you continue to make your way through this book.

Chapter 3: Employment Versus Self-Employment

People looking to make the jump from employee to business owner often ask me questions about the dangers involved.

"What do I do if my business doesn't work out?"

"How did you work up the courage to quit your job?"

Questions like these stem from the idea that there is safety and stability in being employed, and that entrepreneurship is a shot in the dark, which I think is total nonsense. Though this book is written for existing business owners, I still think it's worthwhile to discuss the realities of employment versus self-employment.

I know too many entrepreneurs who waste time and focus eyeing the world of "stable" employment because their business plan hasn't yet panned out. They keep one foot out the door, worried that their business will fail, never realizing that it's their lack of commitment that's holding them back. Knowing the true nature of employment and self-employment can help eliminate this distraction and doubt.

Employment Versus Self-Employment

The Entrepreneurial Evolution

The Safer Side of Business

I know that many people think starting a business is a gamble, but employment is really no safer than self-employment. In fact, I believe that there is a lot more risk involved in working for somebody else.

When you start your own business, you control everything from the number of hours you work to the packaging of the product you sell. You choose who to serve and how much to charge, and you make all of these decisions with your own best interest in mind.

On the other hand, being an employee means giving your boss total control. You give the reins to a business owner who probably prioritizes their own profit. In many cases, you're just a means to an end, and you're highly expendable. If your boss thinks somebody can do your job better than you, you get replaced. If your department is struggling or the company's stock starts to fall, you may be terminated.

I saw the drawbacks of "stable" employment firsthand during the recession of 2008. When the market crashed that year, I was running an application security company. Many of my employed friends were either laid off, or had their salaries slashed. Having trusted their financial futures to employers who were now scrambling to save themselves, my friends were stuck. They wouldn't recover until their employers could right the ship; many waited years while their bosses protected their own interests.

Being a business owner saved me. My application security company died that day and wasn't resuscitated for another 3 years, but I was able to adapt and continue earning more than any of my employed friends.

After one month where we lost twice as many clients as we gained, I knew that business was done for. I met with my business partner, and together we agreed to put it out of its misery. We both knew that nobody would spend money on a virtual protection service in a struggling economy. People were worrying about feeding their families, not app security.

My business partner and I decided to shift our focus to something that suited the current state of the market. We decided to concentrate on inexpensive mobile and web design services. It built off of our existing technical abilities, and took advantage of our understanding of the web development world.

We knew that big companies would need to tighten their budgets, and their expensive web design providers would end up on the chopping block. These companies would shop around for an inexpensive yet high-quality solution, and we would be waiting for them.

While my employed friends struggled to make ends meet from 2008-2011, my mobile and web design company enjoyed its most profitable years to date. Because we were in control, my business partner and I were able to adapt. Our company could stay afloat even during the most uncertain of times. Although our application security business fell, we had the freedom and flexibility we needed to change our entire model. Within two weeks, we had a promising new business venture up and running.

Starting your own business gives you greater security, adaptability, and earning potential than you'll ever have as an employee. The safety and stability the general public sees in traditional employment is an illusion.

But if that's true, then who is creating this illusion, and why? It's simple: there are people out there who want to make money off of you, and spreading misinformation serves their interests.

I can give you a great example from the financial industry. Has anybody ever told you that mutual funds are a great investment?

People generally accept the notion that mutual funds are a safe option, but the real experts will tell you otherwise. I promise you that any high-level financial guru you meet will have a total of zero mutual fund investments in their portfolio. Still, bank managers and mutual fund investors will look you in the eye and tell you they're a smart move.

Why are bank managers passing incorrect information off as "common knowledge"? Obviously, they want you to invest. Banks endorse mutual funds because they profit off of the investments, just like big business owners endorse employment because they profit off of your work.

You may hear lifelong employees and long-term mutual fund investors talking about how happy they are with their decisions, and I'm truly glad for them if that's the case. However, I can tell you that ego influences how we perceive our experiences; after 20 years of employment or investment in a weak mutual fund, it can be tough to admit there were better options out there.

Of course, being self-employed is not for everyone. Some people simply don't want to start their own business, and there's nothing wrong with that, so long as the decision is made for the right reasons. Don't let misinformation discourage you from your dreams of being a business owner – if you do it right, it can be a lot safer than you think.

A Safe Start-Up Strategy

If you're unsure whether self-employment is right for you, I suggest you ask yourself the following two questions:

1. Am I self-motivated? Self-employment requires a lot of drive and discipline; if you can't be productive without someone peering over your shoulder, this path isn't right for you. No business book in the world will help you if you're not hungry.

2. Do I believe in myself? There may be times in your career where your plans are delayed, deals are lost, or money is mismanaged. You'll need courage and self-belief to work through these trying times.

Since you're reading this book, I'll assume you answered these questions in the affirmative. You have the drive inside you required to be successfully self-employed.

If you're on the verge of launching your first business, I have some advice to help you smooth the transition. Whether you're looking to start your own business or expand an existing one, you should know that there's a safe approach - it just takes a little patience, and a lot of work.

What if I told you that you could launch your business tomorrow, risk-free? It sounds impossible, but it's very simple.

All you need to do is start working during the evening after your day job ends. It's the perfect opportunity to build your side business without affecting your income. It's an obvious solution that often hides in plain sight.

Some people can't stand the thought of working again after commuting home at the end of an eight-hour day, but it's not as difficult as it sounds. Remember that you are stronger than you think - keep your "suffering" in perspective. You're a human being, and you're only here because you're a descendent in a long line of survivors. The "discomfort" of a few hours extra work in your comfy home is bearable, and it will be well-worth the chance to field test your business with nothing at stake.

Within 6 months, you'll know whether or not your business idea will work, and can either quit your job to pursue the business full-time, or stay right where you are.

I use this safety-first startup strategy all the time. It's how I got the book you're reading off the ground.

Let's say that you want to be an independent mechanic. Your current day job ends at 5PM. Go home, eat dinner, and unwind with your family for an hour or so. At some point before you go to bed that night, push out 4 hours of work on your business, and see if it pays off over the next 6 months.

If you're a real pro, your prices will be better than what people find at auto shops, and the service will surpass anything they'd find at a dealership. You'll have positive results.

After six months, you will definitely see whether your business is worth pursuing. If your 4-hour commitment is making good money, and your day job is keeping you from meeting the demand of your side business, it's time - you can wave goodbye to your boss, and officially start your own company. If six months have passed with little result, you can either regroup and try another idea, or start enjoying free evenings again after work. Either way, you tried, and you'll have an idea whether or not self-employment is right for you.

I know that it's tough to pull the trigger on full-time self-employment. Quieting your doubts will be one of your biggest challenges. Your mind will play tricks on you; you'll convince yourself that those six months of success were a case of beginner's luck, and that your profits are unsustainable. What if the market changes entirely?

Try to breathe, and remember that self-employment gives you many more recovery options and escape hatches than your day job.

Imagine that your independent mechanic business has been booming for the past 4 years. Suddenly, you see that the market is shifting as the demand for electric cars begins to grow.

As the business owner, you're prepared for this shift. You're involved with the daily process, and have done enough market research to have anticipated this big change. You can gradually begin transitioning into the electric car industry. Once the shift occurs, you will be ready with all of the licenses and certificates you need to accommodate this new demand, and can seamlessly enter into a profitable new market.

Contrast this scenario with that of an auto shop employee. This employee tunes out the automotive industry when he punches out every night at 5PM. Why would he pay attention to the shifts of a market over which he has no control?

When electric cars take over the market, the employed mechanic is doomed. He is completely blindsided by the change, alerted only once business dries up and his boss lets him go. He now lacks worthwhile skills in the new electric car market, and is in trouble, alongside all of his mechanic friends. Unless he starts upgrading his skills, all he can do is start handing out resumes and searching for somebody else to put his faith in.

These kinds of market shifts happen all of the time, and many industries have been wiped out over the course of economic history. When this happens, employees start from scratch, and employers adjust.

Who would you rather be in this scenario?

The Bottom Line

The bottom line is that being your own boss is much safer and more stable than being an employee. You will earn more, remain flexible in ever-changing markets, and retain control of your financial future as a business owner. I can tell you from experience that no one will want you to succeed more than you.

Transitioning into self-employment doesn't have to be a gamble. Try my safe start-up method. Don't lose perspective; remind yourself that this doubled workload is only temporary, and make sure to take some time to relax in between shifts. If your business is meant to be, you are about to enter an exciting new chapter of your life. You can do this.

Chapter 4:
Keep It In Perspective

I have known many business owners whose main problem boiled down to perspective.

Today, we live in a culture that expects instant gratification. Our instincts to seek immediate satisfaction were meant to help us survive, but they've made us indulgent. We want what we want when we want it, and have advanced society to the point where this is actually possible. Within seconds of the thought popping into your head, you can order almost anything online. Social media gives us instant feedback on our pictures, art, and opinions. Drive-through menus, dating apps, and emergency dialers put food, love, and personal protection at our fingertips every second of the day.

Until very recently, instant gratification was basically unheard of. Today, we normalize food, water, shelter, and security, but these were luxuries that few had access to. Surviving took up most of our time and effort. We like to talk about how we work hard today, but it's a joke compared to what people have gone through for most of human history.

People have become too used to getting things with minimal effort. We struggle to keep things in proportion, and lose touch with the relationship between work and results. Working and waiting for something you want is definitely hard, but it's important; unfortunately, this has become quite rare in our culture of convenience. Being too used to life's luxuries sounds like a great problem to have, but when you really think about it, easy living and entitlement have destroyed more potential businesses than greed, corruption, and con-artists combined.

You need to keep things in proportion if you are going to succeed as an entrepreneur. This basic concept needs to be understood before we move any further. If you want to be able to stand up to the challenges your business will face, you need to know exactly what you're made of. Some people have forgotten where they came from, or stopped appreciating what they have.

In this chapter, I share two exercises I use to keep the things in my life in proportion. These exercises have the potential to change the wiring of your day-to-day thinking. They will challenge the limits you put on yourself, give you a new appreciation for life, and protect you from personal compromise.

Thinking Back in Time

For the first exercise, you need to remember how things used to be. You don't have to go far – thinking back a few centuries is all it takes to really hammer this point home.

Imagine waking up shivering every day. There is no electricity. You're damp from the rain. If you're lucky, you have a thatched roof over your head, but shelter isn't guaranteed. Your neighbours either live in mud huts, or sleep under the stars.

You're starving. If you're lucky, you've saved a stale hunk of bread for breakfast. If not, your day will be spent working for food. You'll pass your waking hours toiling in a field, pushing yourself to the breaking point knowing your family's lives are on the line. Whether you farm or hunt, every meal has its cost-efficiency considered. You have to be sure the meal will be worth the calories you'll spend to get it, or you're dead. There is no welfare safety net to help you; there is barely a society to speak of here, so don't expect social assistance.

Your personal security is always on the line. Your family is never safe, and you can never let your guard down. Invaders could charge over the horizon any second. Bands of thieves or the armies of the neighbouring feudal lord could storm your home without warning, destroying everything you love. If people don't take you out, plagues might.

Even the most basic things like washing your clothes, going to the toilet, or getting a drink of water is a thousand times more difficult than what you're used to today.

When you practice this exercise, remember how hard life was, but more importantly, remember that people endured. Despite these incredible challenges, human beings made progress. Even during a period where fundamental human needs were rarely being met, and every day was a struggle to survive, people prevailed. Art, culture, architecture, music, philosophy, science, and commerce all grew out of conditions we would call unbearable.

It didn't happen overnight, and it wasn't easy. People prevailed because they worked, struggled, and pushed their limits to overcome terrible obstacles.

Why is this realization important? Why bother with this exercise?

There will be times in your personal and professional life where you will feel as though you've hit your ceiling. You try your best, but things don't work out as planned. It's all so much harder than you imagined. Your goal seems beyond your reach; maybe your business plan aimed too high? You regroup and try again, but the amount of work ahead seems impossible.

This is the point where most people quit or rethink their approach in hopes of finding an easier path. Resist the urge to abandon your plan, unless you really messed up and overlooked something obvious the first time around.

Trying something easier won't bring you any closer to your goal. You might be able to convince yourself that you're making a strategic adjustment, but you're really just compromising. This is the problem of perspective and proportionality that victimizes business owners every day, but it doesn't have to be this way!

In this culture of instant gratification, we are much less willing to put in the time. We have a very low threshold for hard work, and an unreal expectation for how it's supposed to pay off. If we don't keep things in proportion, we are generally less prepared to work hard.

Thinking back on how things used to be can help. It reminds us that people were tough, and capable of more than we might think. You can carry much more weight on your shoulders than you know, as long as you do it with a smile. Human history is full of hard workers, and you should count yourself among them.

Morning Affirmations

The second exercise I use is more of a routine. I start every day with what I call my "morning affirmations."

In the Hebrew Bible, there is something called the "Morning Blessings." The reading is about three pages long, filled with basic blessing that are written to put your life in proportion. Each is truly amazing by itself, and reading them in their entirety starts my day on the right foot regardless of what problems await me in the office.

As I said, these blessings are extremely basic. The first reads: "Thank you God for giving me my eyesight." This is so simple that it almost seems trivial, until you really think about it. When I woke up this morning, I could see. That is incredible. Many people are not so lucky.

The second blessing thanks God for the ability to dress yourself. There are people in the world who depend on others for this basic thing.

The third thanks God for the ability to go to the washroom independently. There are people in the world who rely on special tubs when nature calls, but you're not one of them. Are you really going to let a bad meeting or missed sale bring you down?

The list goes on, but you get the idea. These basic Morning Blessings help give me perspective. They put my problems in proportion. By the time I've reached page three, life seems great. I feel so fortunate. All of my problems seem small and within my power to fix. Even if my office building is on fire, I start my day knowing that 99% of my life is on the right track.

You don't need to read the Morning Blessings specifically. You only need to remind yourself of everything you have. Positive affirmations come in many different forms. The more basic they seem, the better.

The Bottom Line

The bottom-line lesson here is that you need to keep everything in perspective. The exercises outlined here can help. No problem that you encounter in your business career will be harder than what your ancestors faced, or what thousands of less fortunate people deal with every day. Remember that people are tough, and you're a person. In doing so, you won't only be able to achieve more, but you'll be able to do it with a smile, without compromising the harmony between your family and business. Much of the stress melts away when you realize that while you may be pushing yourself, you're nowhere near the brink.

There will be many lessons in this book that will be "easier read than done." They'll make sense when you read them, but when you try to apply them to your life, you'll find that you're pushed far out of your comfort zone. I hope that after reading this chapter, you will not allow yourself to give up. Remember that you'll never realize your full potential unless you're willing to push past the limitations you've placed on yourself. As my army commander used to say: "Anytime you feel like you've given it 100%, it means you have another 75% in the tank." I've tested the wisdom of these words many times, and never found it wanting.

Keep It In Perspective

"Anytime you feel like you've given it 100%, it means you have another 75% in the tank."

Biplov'16

The Entrepreneurial Evolution

Chapter 5:
Don't Dwell On the Past

Don't Dwell on the Past

Biplov'16

The Entrepreneurial Evolution

While managing the vendors, owners, and staff of multiple businesses, I've had many opportunities to interact with new people, and crossed paths with all different personality types. Over the years, these interactions have shown me a great deal of human diversity, and they've also shown me ways we're all the same.

One thing that we all seem to have in common is regret. Almost everyone I encounter has some sort of distressing past that they wish was in their power to change. The time I've spent listening to other people's regrets is substantial; I can only imagine how many hours (and opportunities) those people lost agonizing over their personal histories.

Regret doesn't confine itself to the past; a single mistake can hound you for your whole career. I've watched business owners pass up excellent opportunities because of a bad experience they had twenty years earlier. It's quite natural to avoid something that has burned you or a loved one before - this is the same survival instinct that teaches children not to touch red-hot stove elements twice - but it's a base instinct that modern entrepreneurs have to evolve past. Rather than avoiding the heat altogether, we want to learn how to use it to cook our next meal!

A very smart man changed the way I manage my regret and my business with the following story. I hope it has the same effect on you.

The Weight of Regret

A priest and his student were preparing to cross a river on the journey back to their village. As the priest began to lower himself into the water, his student noticed a woman nearby. She was half-dressed in damp clothes.

"Will you help me cross?" the woman asked.

The priest agreed to help, took her onto his back, and made his way to the other side. His student followed sheepishly, averting his eyes from the woman's partially exposed form. The woman thanked the priest as she left, and the clergymen carried on towards the village in silence.

Three months later, the student looked to the priest and said: "I must ask a question that has been bothering me for some time." The priest smiled and gave the student his full attention.

"Do you remember the woman who climbed on your back as we crossed the river?" The priest nodded, and the student continued. "How could you let her touch you in such a way? She was barely clothed. It violates everything you have taught me."

In that moment, the priest noticed the worry creasing his student's face, and the bags under his eyes.

"Ah, my boy," the priest said through a knowing smile. "I carried that woman across the river for thirty seconds, and you've been carrying her for three months."

This story probably isn't the first warning you've heard about harbouring regret. It's surprising how many people fall into this trap, considering how many cultural teachings and clichés we deploy against it. There is an old Arab proverb that suggests we write the bad thoughts in the sand so that they can be easily erased. Buddha tells us: "Do not dwell in the past, do not dream of the future, concentrate the mind on the present moment." Tony Robbins made a career out of helping people realize that "the past does not equal the future." There are countless other examples.

Still, despite all their warnings, we let our pasts control us. Have you ever walked away from a project thinking "I'm never working with _____ again!" I've seen business owners swear off everything from web marketing to foreign outsourcing based on a single bad experience. Ego gets involved, and they tell everyone who'll listen that the resource that burned them is a scam. The experience becomes highly negative; not only are they dwelling on a painful memory and shunning a useful resource, they're also denying themselves an opportunity for personal growth.

There's a better way!

Make Your Mistakes Work For You

Dwelling in the painful memory of a mistake does nothing for you. When I'm angry, I drive to the gym and make that aggressive energy work for me. You need to channel the pain of your past in a similarly productive way.

If you are one of those people that dwell on the past, then my advice to you is to take an hour or two to analyze the situation in full. Pour over your bad experience and gather all of the feedback you can. The sting of failure is an excellent motivator; you'll attack this brainstorm session with gusto. Once you have mined the experience for all it is worth, acknowledge that it belongs in the past, and proceed in your life. Write it in the sand, and let it blow away.

The value of this approach is twofold. First, you'll learn something about whatever it was that failed you in the past. Instead of wasting time poking at an open wound, you deepen your understanding of something business-related. Maybe you'll realize that you chose the wrong kind of web marketing company, and were focusing too much on the quantity of traffic rather than the quality. Maybe your mistake wasn't choosing to outsource work, but rather paying your foreign freelancer up front in full. Asking yourself some simple questions about why the initiative failed will yield some important lessons that will help you in the future.

Secondly, and perhaps more importantly, this approach is cathartic. The brainstorm session is a great opportunity to get things off of your chest. You turn a negative into a positive, and stop knotting up your insides over your mistake. Your past becomes constructive instead of destructive.

Let me give you an example of this approach in action. I see a lot of business owners haunted by their experiences with the stock market, so why not start there?

No matter who's telling it, I always hear the same story about stock market regret: someone invested everything they had, and then lost it all. It's always presented to me as a tragic case of bad luck, when it should be looked at as a lesson. Rather than taking an opportunity to improve their process and refine their market strategies, these business owners torture themselves for their mistakes, and swear off a useful investment vehicle.

Instead of agonizing over their failure for the rest of their life, let's imagine one of these business owners applied my approach. The business owner wakes up the day after their stock market catastrophe and plans two hours of their day to analyze the situation in full.

During the brainstorm session, the business owner asks themselves some tough questions:

1. Did I really have a proper understanding of the stock market before I made my move? Did I take the time to educate myself on stock options at a proper school, and build my confidence on a test trading account for at least a year?

2. Was it really smart to put all of my money into a single investment vehicle (especially one as risky as the stock market)?

3. Was it in my best interest to rely on 3rd party advice?

The answers to these simple questions offer some important lessons. In this case, the business owner learns first that they need to be highly educated before entering the stock market. Next, they realize that cannot invest everything into one market; smart investors spread their money in real estate, bonds, stocks, and shares in real companies. Finally, they learn to question the value of 3rd party stock picks - if the broker's advice was so good, don't you think he would invest all of his money in the picks you are paying him for?

The brainstorm session ends, and the business owner feels a weight off their shoulders. They've armed themselves with knowledge for another run at the stock market, treating the experience as a learning resource rather than a regret.

It is unquestionably better to approach your past mistakes in this way. It doesn't matter whether you're dwelling on lost love or a missed investment opportunity; rather than reliving the pain of your loss indefinitely, deepen your understanding with a simple one-time analysis, and then use that knowledge to move on to bigger and better things.

The Bottom Line

The bottom-line here is that we cannot dwell on the past. Our mistakes should work for us, not control us. Torturing yourself for years will only bring more failure - learn from it, let go, and move towards life's next big opportunity.

Chapter 6: Building Positive Experiences

Build Positive Experiences

The Entrepreneurial Evolution

Have you ever wondered what makes someone who they are?

Many years ago, a friend of mine described the nature of personal identity as "a collection of successes and failures." She was siding with nurture over nature in that eternal argument; in her opinion, your character is formed largely by past experiences.

The more I thought about this idea, the more it seemed to be true. Life experiences impart life lessons, which inform the values and behaviours that make us who we are. Presumably, those with more negative experiences, or "failures," would be meek, angry, or insecure, while "successful" people would have more confidence and creativity; it's exactly what business gurus, life coaches, and fight trainers mean when they talk about a "winner's mentality." And it's the reason why you can't dwell on your failures.

Some people are convinced that a "winner's mentality" is something you're born with, but I disagree. You can be born with a strong spirit, but you can also build one by creating positive experiences.

Building A Winner's Mentality In Others

How would your business and family life improve if you knew how to cultivate confidence?

Building a winner's mentality is easy - you just have to make sure your collection of successes is larger than your collection of failures. This is done by building positive experiences, either for yourself or for others.

Let me give you an example of how this is done:

Let's suppose that John needs his house painted. He asks his son for help, seeing the chore as an opportunity to pass along some painting skills, and build his confidence up.

John knows that in order to get the desired results, he needs to set his son up for success. He takes his time to explain the job thoroughly, outlining a simple task that he knows his son can handle. He creates a simple plan: John will be responsible for the majority of the work, while his son will be in charge of painting the window frames.

John makes sure his son has the tools and knowledge he needs to do well. He demonstrates a proper brush stroke, and shows him how to get proper coverage without marking the glass. He stays close to provide support and answer any questions that might arise.

Given everything he needs to excel, John's son does a great job. After a few hours, the window frames are finished with an even, drip-free coat of blue. The project is a big success; John got an enthusiastic helper for the day, and his son enjoyed a positive experience.

John rigged the game so that everyone wins. His house is painted, and his son feels like a winner. It's important to note that John was trying to give his son an experience, not score free labour. The task he assigned was meant to help his son grow, not make John's life easier. He kept his endgame in mind, and executed the plan flawlessly.

Across town, Luke has also recruited his son to help him with a house-painting chore. John and Luke take very different approaches to the day's work, despite their sons being the same age, and having the same inexperience.

Luke isn't thinking about building a positive experience - he's just thinking about painting his house as quickly and efficiently as possible. He reasons that the fastest way to get the job done is to start on opposite ends, then meet in the middle. He hands his son a brush, rattles off some quick instruction, and they begin.

Luke's son has never painted before, and he quickly finds himself overwhelmed. His dad is out of sight around the corner, and he's in a big hurry; asking more questions will only slow the day's work down. He decides to try his best, hoping to make his father proud.

It doesn't take long for Luke's son to realize that he's done a poor job. He can see bad brush marks and runs on the siding, and there are flecks of paint on the window panes. When he meets his father at the halfway point, the difference in their work is obvious. Luke tries to mask his disappointment, but it's useless; the damage is done. It gets even worse if Luke tells his son how poorly he did.

Luke didn't think things through, and set his son up for failure. He's left with a frustrated son and a poorly painted house.

The effects of these kinds of negative experiences are long-lasting, impacting our development, character, and potential. Luke's son will have a very different association with painting than John's. There's a chance that he may never want to paint again. But this one incident will impact his life in many more ways than that.

Being deprived of positive experiences in life is a big problem. Failure weighs heavily on people, and it can be very harmful to our self-concept in large doses. They say that experience is the best teacher, and a lifetime of negative lessons can really hurt your outlook. We become afraid to interact with others, try new things, or explore unfamiliar ideas, because experience has shown us that we will fail, lose, or hurt. We develop a "loser's mentality."

I believe that a winner's mindset is within reach of anyone. John didn't do the impossible, he just showed a little forethought, kept the endgame in mind, and jumped on the chance to turn a menial chore into a life-changing experience.

As a father of three, I often feel as though it's my duty to create positive experiences that help my family grow together. One of the best ways I've found is to ask my children for help, just like John did.

Before you can build positive experiences for your children, you need to identify their strengths. Your child might be a natural athlete, a math whiz, or a charismatic joke-teller; every kid is different. Give them something they can excel at, and steer them away from failure early on. Once they've experienced success, they'll have built the mental strength needed to learn some of life's harder lessons. You'll have given them a rock-solid self-concept that will carry them through any future failures.

This can all be applied in the workplace, of course. You can build your employees up in the same way, using progressive challenges to affirm their belief in themselves. The same principles apply. Know your employees' strengths, and give them tasks that are appropriate for their level. It won't take long to develop a company roster of winners.

Building a Winner's Mentality For Yourself

Failed sales meetings, expansions, and partnerships happen all of the time - how do you build positive experiences for yourself when failures are part of business life?

The trick to building a winning business is to welcome failures. As you read in the previous chapter, you need to make them work for you. Embrace your failures as positive experiences.

Your terminology is critical here. I recommend dropping the word "failure" from your business vocabulary altogether. Failure is too final; it implies that we have stopped trying. I prefer to call unsuccessful business interactions "lessons." This simple change of vocabulary can cause a paradigm shift, making stepping stones out of bankruptcy, lost deals, and bad partners. You take the pressure and finality out of every interaction, and rob negative energy of its power.

Treating a failure as a lesson can be difficult to do when ego is involved. Try to remove yourself from the equation, and assess the situation as a cold, third-party observer. Imagine that you've been hired as a consultant to pinpoint what went wrong.

Let me give you an example. Let's say that you just let yourself down at work. You were sure you'd nail that meeting, but wow - what a disaster. The client looked bored, and you noticed them thumbing their phone awake a few times during your presentation. Everything went wrong, and you lost the deal.

Naturally, you're upset. The meeting ends, and your ego is in shambles. You feel doubtful, embarrassed, and even a touch of self-loathing. How do you handle it?

You have two options.

The first option is to dwell on your failure. You can chastise yourself until the end of time. Why didn't you research your client more? Why didn't you have that second cup of coffee? Why would you wear that tie? You'll find no shortage of things to hate yourself for.

This strange impulse to self-flagellate is completely natural, but entirely unproductive, as we discussed in Chapter 5. Do you think you'll be winning clients over, pushing for innovation, and manifesting your dreams while you're busy torturing yourself? Of course not. Every new meeting, idea, or business proposal that you engage during this "mourning" period will be a wasted effort.

The other option is to use your unsuccessful interaction as a positive learning experience. Don't take it personally - I mean this literally and figuratively. Separate yourself entirely from the loss, and look at the interaction through the eyes of an objective observer. Treat it like somebody else's mistake, and analyze where they went wrong.

I like to write down everything I would change about the interaction while it's still fresh in my mind. This allows me to fully absorb the lesson, and it's also a powerful kind of catharsis. There's something special about writing down your thoughts, especially the negative ones. Once your worries are on paper, it feels as though your mind no longer needs to carry them. Writing out your thoughts also forces you to focus on what truly needs to change. You articulate specific problems, rather than letting your doubts spiral, warp, and fester in your mind. The negativity is bled out of the experience with every line of ink you sink into the page. Now, the "failure" is forced to work for you - it's a lesson you can use to plan your next attack.

I've experimented with both options over the course of my career. When I first started in sales, my closing ratio was low-to-average, and I was constantly dwelling on my "failures." I was closing at a rate of 10-15%, which was standard. Yet I felt like a failure because of the high expectations I had for myself. I wanted to improve, but every unsuccessful sale took a toll on me, and there were many.

Eventually, I got sick of crying about my losses. All of that belly-aching wasn't getting me anywhere. During my martial arts career, I wouldn't whine about what a terrible fighter I was after a defeat; I'd show up at the gym on Monday morning and recommit myself to my training. Losses were opportunities to see my flaws. Why was this any different?

The same mindset I relied on to carry me through my martial arts days would also serve me here. I embraced the idea of being a lifelong student of the game. I accepted that I knew very little about sales, and even less about people. Nobody had taught me how to sell or run a business. I was relying entirely on hard work, life experience, and confidence to carry me through. Moving forward, I decided that I would learn something from every business experience I had.

After a few years of consistent failure, I had stockpiled quite a wealth of "lessons" to review. Pouring over my sales history as an objective, third-party observer, I noticed that all of my success came from the clients I felt comfortable with. If I looked back at my sales stats, this meant I was connecting with 10-15% of my clients on a personal level. The solution seemed obvious: I had to learn how to connect with the other 85%.

I started reading everything I could find about making connections with people. I read many business books, but couldn't find the answers I was looking for, so I decided to explore the world of Kabbalah and Chinese philosophy. I saw some progress, but the journey was nowhere near finished. I was better equipped to deal with different personalities, but the work had only just begun. I spent the next 10 years analyzing my unsuccessful interactions and studying social engineering.

Today, my closing rate sits between 70-80%. Granted, it has been a long process, but my progress hasn't stopped. Once you realize that there is always room to improve, dwelling on mistakes seems like a tremendous waste. There are always positive experiences to be built instead.

The Bottom Line

You should always look to build positive experiences, for your family, your employees, and yourself. This is how you cultivate a winner's mentality.

Understand what family members and employees are capable of, and assign them tasks you know they can accomplish. Treat them like talented prospects in the fight game; build them up slowly with progressively greater challenges, and they'll soon develop into champions.

Building positive experiences for yourself is all about your perspective. Remember that negative energy is not always bad; like some cosmic catapult, negative energy works best when it first pulls you in the opposite direction of where you want to go. Some of the watershed moments in my career came out of the darkest times of my life. I would never have climbed so high without having experienced such miserable lows. Negativity is the great equalizer that guides us towards positivity, in the same way that sadness etches out the true joy of happiness in our minds.

You must assess your unsuccessful interactions with the eyes of an objective observer. Remove the word "failure" from your vocabulary, and remember that the outcome is not important so long as the lesson is learned. Know your endgame, create a plan, take action, learn your lesson, and start the cycle all over again as a newly-improved you. The results of your action don't matter as long as you're getting better every time.

Chapter 7: Through Fire is the Spirit Forged

Especially early on in your business career, the siren of success can be dangerous. Novelty and beginners lucky can buoy a business for a while when it's really a sinking ship. It's easy to feel invincible when you're closing deals from the get-go, but you don't learn much; in fact, many people succeed for a while despite their process, not because of it. It's much better to make your mistakes early, lest they catch up with you when it really matters.

Like the mixed martial artist, the businessman learns most from a loss. Nothing highlights holes in your game like a thorough beating. A boxer with a string of knockouts may feel like the baddest man on the planet until a wrestle scoops his legs out from under him and reminds him just how far his game has to evolve. Taking one on the chin with your business can be the greatest gift you ever receive, so long as you are open to the lessons you're being taught.

Lucky for you, I am no stranger to spectacular failure. The business world has bloodied my nose and swollen both my eyes shut. I've absorbed many hits in my life, recovered, and internalized their lessons so that you don't have to. My first real business experience provides a perfect example.

My First Business Experience

After my military service concluded, I opened a pet shop. It seemed like a good idea at the time. I had always loved animals, and felt that I could run this kind of business for the rest of my life.

I was wrong, of course - the pet shop was a tremendous failure that threw me into serious debt. Though I was forced to close my doors less than six months in, it was the best business experience I could have hoped for. I learned four valuable lessons.

Before I opened my pet shop, I was convinced that I'd thought of everything. I had poured over potential locations to find a spot that was convenient for locals yet far from any competition. I invested in a very strong inventory, deciding on a good mix of products and services that I knew people would like. The shop had everything you can think of: fish, dogs, cats, birds, reptiles, rabbits, food, supplies, and even an in-house groomer (me). I told everyone I knew about my shop, and invited them to come celebrate my grand opening with a street party I planned to host out front. I called in favours, explored unfamiliar branches in my family tree, and pressured my friends to try and get as many people there as possible.

Opening day was a huge success. I convinced hundreds of people to come, and many more were drawn in to my shop by the sight of the crowd gathered there. I handed out hundreds of business cards and spoke with smiling visitors as they played with the animals, and by the end of the day I knew things were good. I had gotten the word out, and even made a few sales in the process.

The next month was intoxicating. The siren of success was whispering in my ear and I was listening to her every word. I made lots of sales and had great interactions with my local market. At the end of a profitable day's work, I would wrap up some deliveries, collect payments from my clients, and come home with more money than I could count. I had some great business interactions before then, but never on this scale. "This is what success looks like," I thought. "I've finally made it."

By the second month, I was invincible. Sales grew even

more, and there seemed to be no end in sight. I could not expect the beating that was coming my way because the business world had yet to put up a fight. Little did I know that I was running straight into a knockout punch.

Through Fire is the Spirit Forged

The Entrepreneurial Evolution

My mistakes came to light at the end of the second month when the vendors came to my store looking to be paid. Around this same time, the rent and new taxes were due, along with a slew of other expenses.

I couldn't believe how quickly my bank balance dissolved. I was broke before I had paid back even half of what I owed.

As you can imagine, the pet shop collapsed, closing a few months later and leaving me over $100,000 in debt, back when that amount could buy you a nice house with a beautiful car in the garage.

I had no idea where I'd gone wrong. The siren of success had lured me out to sea and drowned me without warning.

Looking back now, my mistakes seem painfully obvious. After a strong start, I had committed four of the biggest blunders that a business owner can make:

1. I started to advertise like crazy, hoping to increase sales without any real plan in place. With no clear objectives in mind for my marketing campaign, I deferred to the advertisers, whose only goal was to sell me big packages. Years later, I look back at the advertisers I worked with and realize that none of them had any clue about real marketing. They were into self-promotion, not sales promotion.

2. I didn't manage the money my business was generating. I thought that all of the profit was mine - WRONG! The business was generating that money, and I was there to manage it, not to spend it. Instead, I ran out and celebrated my "success" with expensive purchases.

3. I sold the product without the proper markup. I was making something like 10-15% profit on my products, which was nowhere near what I needed to handle the cost of rent, electricity, water, and employee wages.

4. I had no end-game in mind. I hadn't set a goal for the end of the month, and no real notion of what success looked like.

Though I had run my business into ruin, all was not lost. Even then, I had a strong spirit and a learner's mindset, cultivated by years in the military and the martial arts. Some people would break in that situation, buried in debt with their dreams dashed, but I chose to learn from my mistakes instead. I decided to use this setback as a positive learning experience, reinforcing the winner's mentality I outlined in the previous chapter.

I was determined to pay off what I owed within a year. I looked for a job and found an opening as a garbage collector. It was a lesson in humility that I will never forgot. The job was available right away, and though I had thought of it as a serious step down, I swallowed my pride and took the position. It turned out better than I expected. It wasn't time consuming, and it paid quite well.

My next lesson was in resourcefulness. On its own, a garbage collector's wage wouldn't do. I had to find something to take advantage of the free time this position granted me; I started at 2:00AM, and was free by 10:00AM. Before the army, I had earned a massage certification, though I had never found a way to put it to much use. Now, with my back against the wall, I had to make something of it.

The answer was massage parties. I gathered a few massage therapists, and together we visited different gyms, clubs, and companies to host these events. We gave massages to the patrons, and they tipped well, adding to the great wages the business owners were paying us.

However, the real value of these parties came from the advertising opportunities they provided. I had learned from my aimless advertising mistakes, and approached these parties intending to build relationships and earn recognition. I met many long-term clients at these events, and as my roster grew, I began to consider opening a massage school.

Eventually, my father gave me his commercial property to use as my academy. People knew me from my work at massage parties; new students and clients trickled in steadily, and I was able to team up with a big-name school that gave me a valuable boost.

Within twenty-four months of my pet store shutting down, I was debt free. Two years earlier, I had suffered a knockout blow to my bank account and my self-esteem, but I did not let it beat me, even when I missed my goal of paying off my debt within a year. Though I had only tasted success until then, I welcomed adversity as an old friend, embracing my failures and paying close attention to their teachings. My business mind evolved, learning lessons in humility, resourceful, and four vital errors to avoid as a business owner. I chose to build a positive experience.

The Bottom Line

The bottom-line here is simple: if you take nothing more from this chapter, remember that you always learn the most from a loss. You can't spot your mistakes when you're drunk on success. Any setback you face should be treated as a chance to build your winner's mindset; failures are just opportunities to evolve.

Chapter 8:
Put Your Ego Aside and Make the Move

When I was a kid, I wanted a date with the prettiest girl in school. I saw her every day, but I couldn't muster up the courage to ask her out. I didn't think she would say yes, so I didn't try.

My dad noticed the way I was admiring her while picking me up from school one day, and decided to give me some advice. He wanted me to ask her to the upcoming school dance. He told me two things as I sat in the car all flushed:

1. "Everybody feels the way you do about that girl. Nobody is asking her to the dance because they're all convinced she's too good for them. She needs to choose somebody, so why not make the first move?"

2. "If she says no, nothing will have changed. She isn't your girlfriend now, so what do you have to lose?"

I was quiet on the drive home. I spent the rest of that night thinking over what he had told me.

Today, I am diligent about planning before making big business moves, and I had the same mentality as a boy. I made sure to aim before I took my shot.

I exhausted every possibility as I played the conversation out in my head planning that night. I sometimes pictured myself saying just the right thing, creasing her face with a smile, and sweeping her off her feet. More often, I saw myself tripping over my words and firing flecks of spit into her face as I spoke. I could already feel my face redden at the thought of my friends watching me fail. Would she smile shyly, shrink away, or throw herself into my arms?

Put Your Ego Aside and Make the Move

Biplov'16

The Entrepreneurial Evolution

After a long night, I felt I had prepared an answer for every possible reaction. I decided that I was going to do it.

I woke up the next morning with fluttering in my chest and sweaty palms, but I knew what I had to do. I was on a mission as I walked to school that day. I would ask her the moment I saw her.

As I arrived at school, I saw her standing with a few friends in the soccer field before the first bell had rung. I steeled my nerves as best I could, then started across the field. I remember pulling my shoulders back and wearing my best casual look as I made my way to her. Her friends stared at me, unimpressed, but I brushed them off. I kept my target in focus until we were face to face. This was the moment I had been waiting for.

She rejected me almost before I could finish getting the question out of my mouth. Still, my father was right: I hadn't really lost anything by asking. What had I even been afraid of in the first place? The fear I felt fluttering in my chest was just my ego scrambling for self-preservation. 35 years later, I still wrestle with my ego, and I still lean on the advice my father gave me to overcome it.

The lesson here reaches well beyond elementary school romance. Business owners deal with this problem every day, myself included. In fact, the more businesses I get involved with, the more business owners I see paralyzed by fear when they should be pulling the trigger.

Self-Preservation or Self-Destruction?

Some business owners are controlled by ego. Afraid of failure or rejection, they miss opportunities, or pay to outsource work that they could have easily done themselves.

Here's one scenario I see playing out quite often when small companies try using a targeted form of cold calling for the first time. Don't be distracted by the subject of this story; maybe you never intend to work with cold calling in your life it's the underlying lesson that matters.

1. The owner of a small company makes a list of businesses he would like to connect with.

2. The owner spends days or even weeks compiling contact details, preferences, and other information. Hours are spent on LinkedIn, Facebook, and business websites trying to learn as much as possible about the companies that will be called.

3. With the contact list complete, the business owner is ready to go. He has everything he needs to connect, introduce himself, and present his offer. Instead, he plans to make the calls the following week. Better to come prepared, he tells himself.

4. The week he had planned on arrives. Suddenly, there is some "important" matter to attend to. Calling the prospects will be delayed for a couple of weeks as other important things keep popping up.

5. Eventually, the business owner hires somebody else to make the calls. He thinks he is too busy, but the reality is that he's afraid of being rejected, like I was with my elementary school crush.

6. A few weeks later, the business owner is frustrated by the poor results his cold calling employee produced. Rather than picking up the phone himself, he will look elsewhere for capable employees. The results will be much the same, however, because the business owner has no real training or advice to impart, since he has no experience with cold calling himself. He cannot properly prepare his employees for a job he hasn't done.

7. Eventually, after a lot of wasted time and money, the business owner decides that cold calling prospects is ineffective. He decides to find a different (and less frightening) approach.

So what happened? In trying to protect his ego, this business owner hurt his business. He took the time to create a plan, but it wasn't enough. He couldn't put his ego aside to make the move that his company needed. Self-preservation turned to self-destruction when ego halted the action that needed to be taken.

What if my father had given this business owner the same advice I'd gotten as a young boy? The business owner is still nervous, but he values results more than his personal comfort level. He can keep his discomfort in perspective. He makes the move his desired results demand.

Frankly, this is how a good business owner operates. A good business owner puts the future and success of their business ahead of the wants of their own ego. The company is bigger than you; though you may be the business owner, you are still employed by the business, and need to work for it as such. You cannot abandon a task that your manager assigns you, even when that manager is you.

So what happens when he does what's right? This brave business owner takes an hour out of his day to populate his cold calling list with 20 promising candidates. With his list ready to go, he calls these 20 people, introduces himself, and makes his offer. He begins his day with no deals, and therefore approaches the cold calling experience knowing he has nothing to lose. Of the 20 people he calls, 2 express that they would be happy to meet. A day later, he has met with both interested parties, and successfully closed a deal with one.

After this experience, the business owner understands that cold calling does work. With a proven method under his belt, he can now pass this knowledge on to his employees. He knows the process inside and out, and can teach new hirees exactly how to get the job done. The company's cold calling system will get results since their training is informed by the boss's real-world experience. The business saves time and money, and will generate many more sales than in the previous scenario, all because the owner put his ego aside and did what needed to be done.

Even if the cold call campaign fails miserably, the business owner who overcame his ego comes out ahead. He will have wasted 3-4 hours of his time in total, rather than the weeks that were lost in the first scenario.

The Bottom Line

The bottom line here is simple: your success depends on your ability to set your ego aside and make the move, whatever that move may be. There are many people out there who need your services, and many competitors who have already quieted their ego and begun to chase down results. Don't confuse hesitation with self-preservation - that's exactly what the competition is hoping for. Create a plan, keep things in perspective, and make the move!

Chapter 9:
Remove Distractions

Distractions are our archenemies, and they're all around us. Noisy air-conditioners, the ceaseless ring of your mobile phone, the heavy breathing of a coworker - anything slowing you down on your way from A to B is a distraction that needs to go.

Any time you are being distracted, it means you are experiencing a loss. Distractions translate to declining productivity, missed sales opportunities, and customer service slip-ups, all of which move you further away from your goals. These must be eliminated if you are going to succeed, but there is a right and wrong way to go about it.

I've come a long way in my personal and professional life because I've learned to pay attention to my surroundings, identify distractions, and remove them in a way that benefits those around me. Today, much of my work consulting with other businesses revolves around finding creative and cost-effective solutions that do the same for them.

In this section, I will share the model of cold analysis, communication, and cooperative action I use. I explain my method using an experience involving the internet, but don't fixate on this one example. I've applied the same formula to eliminate noise pollution, office drama, unprofessional attire, cell phone use, and every other distraction you can imagine in the workplace.

Getting Sucked into the Matrix

For a long time, my family and I were powerless against the distracting power of the internet. A WiFi miasma had spread through our home and sucked the life out of us all. When I could pry myself offline between meals, I would usually find my wife and kids alone in their rooms, completely immersed in their smartphone, computer, or tablet. There was very little interaction; only the faint glow of LED screens creeping into the hallway assured me that my family was home at night. We could hardly bring ourselves to set down our devices long enough to talk over a family meal.

This style of living went against many of the goals my wife and I had set for our family. We all knew how important it was to spend time together, but we were struggling to make it happen.

Once I became aware of this problem, I took a step back and tried to assess the situation as an objective observer. The first thing I noticed was how much of my day was spent online. My ego had me convinced that years in the military and martial arts had given me sure-fire self-discipline, but a cold analysis told me otherwise. The internet was a distraction that I couldn't resist. It was easy to tell myself I was getting work done, but I was really just thumbing through social media feeds, tech reviews, and news sites for hours on end. I added up the hours I was wasting, and the numbers didn't lie.

If I couldn't manage my own internet addiction, how could I expect that kind of restraint from my children? When we called the family to the dinner table, we were competing with never-ending video game requests, news ticker updates, and instant messages from friends. We didn't stand a chance.

Clearly, unlimited internet access was the distraction that had to be removed, but I had to go about it the right way. I could have marched upstairs, snatched the electronics from my wife and children, and locked everybody in a room together, but would that have gotten me the best results? Forcing things would only create chaos. I would become the bad guy and my family would turn against me, ruining the family connection I wanted in the first place.

Instead, my approach was to remove the distraction in a way that was helpful rather than forceful. I had to present the problem to my family so that we were all on the same page, and involve them in the plan. I told them: "Unlimited WiFi time is getting in the way of us being the family we want to be." Once this obstacle was laid out in front of us, we could all see that something had to change, and could start working together.

With everyone in agreement, I bought an outlet timer and installed it on the plug we used to power our router. This gave us access to the internet only during certain predetermined hours each day. The timer was set so that the WiFi would not work for the first hour that my kids arrived home from school. This gave us time to have lunch together and swap stories about our day. An hour later, the outlet would turn on, and the WiFi would activate. We would have two hours of free time before it flicked off again so that the kids could focus on their homework.

This cheap $26 outlet timer worked miracles. A house that had felt uninhabited was now a home filled with laughter, conversation, and play. We disabled the WiFi for certain hours of the weekend, and suddenly my kids and I had no reason to waste the day playing with our phones in bed. Instead, we gathered downstairs to eat and joke as a family. Now, we could enjoy the internet without it ever interfering with our family bond. We achieved our goal, avoided any conflict, and were now closer than ever.

The outlet timer itself is much less important than the underlying approach I used to solve the problem. I had to identify the distraction, understand how it interfered with our goals through dialogue, and apply a solution that would help us all improve. You can apply this process of objective analysis, communication, and cooperative action to manage any distractions your business may be facing.

I used this same approach at my office when the internet was disrupting my employees' productivity (though the specific solution differed). When I checked their browser history, I noticed they spent lots of time on Facebook, YouTube, and other websites unrelated to their work. An objective analysis helped me realize that they weren't slacking off intentionally; after all, I was struggling with the same issue, and nobody cared more about my business than I did. There was no use getting angry, but the distraction still had to be removed if my business were to succeed.

Having identified the problem, it was time to act.

First, I would need my employees to understand that what I was about to do was intended to help them. This was not difficult, since most employees want to be good at their job. Everybody wants to feel respected for their contribution to the company. Nobody really wants to slack off and ride out the clock at work: it's stressful and unrewarding at the end of the day. As we discussed the problem, they agreed that eliminating internet distractions would help them get more done and feel better about themselves.

Now it was time to take cooperative action. I obviously couldn't install an outlet timer at the office since all of our work was done online, but something had to be done. In this case, the answer was to install a "proxy," a device that I could use to filter out any social media, games, or unproductive websites that competed for my employees' attention. Knowing that I was removing the distractions that consumed my employees' time and denied them the rewarding feelings that came from an honest day's work, I was more than happy to cover the cost of the proxy.

In the end, I think the proxy benefited my employees as much as it helped my company. The productivity boost was great, but the mood around the office had brightened, too. My employees felt better about themselves and their work. Gently removing these online distractions helped my employees to focus on their goals, and produced way better results than I would have gotten if I'd been the angry boss.

The Bottom Line

Remove Distractions

Biplov '16

The Entrepreneurial Evolution

The bottom line is that distractions need to be identified and removed properly if your business is going to succeed. The more of them you remove, the more productivity you will gain.

Cold analysis, communication, and cooperative action are key; this approach lets you avoid any conflict, and collaborate to find creative solutions to the unique distractions you face. In the case of the internet addictions I encountered, my family and employees understood that the restrictions were helping us reach our goals, rather than forcing everyone to do things my way - instead of being met with resistance, reluctance, and negative feelings, it was all positive.

Identify the problem, think and discuss how it affects your goals, and work together with those affected to take it down.

Chapter 10: The Mirror

I think the way you look in the mirror says a lot about your chances as a business owner.

Anyone involved in sales interactions or client care must carefully consider how they are presenting themselves to the world. Before people commit to buying your product or hiring your company, they need to feel good about you. To do that, they will literally try to get a sense of who you are. In the same way that we rely on sound, sight, touch, smell, and taste to understand the world around us, the client sitting across from you taps into their senses to get a feel for your business proposal.

We all know that it's what's on the inside that counts, but a heart of gold and a game-changing product are both worthless if your first impressions keep pushing clients away. As human beings, we are programmed to make quick assumptions about people; we receive sensory data, cross-reference it with the context of the situation, and then generate a feeling about whether or not that person is trustworthy. This survival instinct has developed over thousands of years, and it's not going anywhere anytime soon. As much as we'd like to tell ourselves that we have evolved into higher-minded beings, we are still slaves to our most basic senses on some level.

There are ways to use this to your advantage. If you know how to present yourself in a way that appeals to your all client's senses, you guarantee a favourable first impression that sets your proposal up for success.

Appealing to the Client's Senses

The first thing you should do is take a look in the mirror to determine how you look to your client. If tired eyes are looking back at you from under a mop of messy hair, then there's a problem that needs to be addressed.

An unprofessional appearance can really set you back, and that is unacceptable since it's something you can control. You already know what it means to look professional, so why fall short of that image? In the business world, a clean-shaven face or neatly-trimmed beard is always more appealing than one that is scraggly and unkempt, and a suit is more impressive than a t-shirt and shorts.

Appealing to your client's sense of sight has nothing to do with "beauty" or model looks, and it's not about who spent the most money, either. Rather, it's about creating visual indicators of effort, health, and conscientiousness that your client reads in your appearance; they won't care if you paid $20 or $200 for your shirt, but they will notice whether or not it is cleaned and ironed!

You can also easily appeal to your client's sense of smell. Don't worry, I'm not suggesting that you douse yourself in perfume before a big meeting. Appealing to a client's sense of sight does not require that you be "beautiful," and appealing to their sense of smell doesn't mean you have to smell like roses. You just can't smell bad. Freshen up with a shower or some deodorant if you catch a whiff of sweat on yourself before a meeting. If you smoke, resist the urge to light one up before sitting down with a client. Though some smokers enjoy the smell, most people find it offensive. If you meet with a non-smoker while reeking of nicotine, they won't be happy about it, and this tiny detail can make all the difference.

Obviously, you need to appeal to your client's sense of hearing. It goes without saying that you need to know what you're talking about at a sales meeting - if you don't, you can just throw this book out now, because your business is going nowhere. However, knowing your business inside-out is only half the battle. Knowing what to say is useless if you don't know how to say it.

If I project my voice and speak with energy and confidence, the client will take me seriously, and associate my words with leadership, authority, and power. On the other hand, if I speak in a quiet voice and end my statements with question-mark inflections, I sound unsure. I could be pitching the greatest idea in the world, but few would take me seriously - their senses are telling them that I don't know what I'm talking about.

What about taste and touch? While your client probably won't be touching or tasting you during your business proposal, you still have a measure of control over these sensory experiences. Try to reserve a comfortable chair for your client, greet them with a firm handshake, and avoid meeting at a restaurant whose menu you're unsure of. Though the softness of their seat and the quality of their meal won't reflect poorly on you, these things can distract the client, and attach bad feelings to their memory of the interaction.

Even for small meetings that can be done over coffee, I'll lean towards Starbucks over the cheaper chains. It really helps me close deals; the client's positive association with a rich cup of coffee seems to rub off on me. For bigger deals, I'll arrange the meeting at a top-tier steakhouse.

I'm often challenged by peers who think I'm out of my mind spending $100 on a meal without any assurances that the deal with be closed at the end of the night, but it makes perfect sense to me. First of all, meeting at a high-quality restaurant ensures that you have a quiet and comfortable place to talk. Secondly, this kind of upscale treatment is something clients may be used to getting from small businesses, which helps your company stand out. Finally, you're appealing to your client's senses by leaving a good taste in their mouth (both figuratively and literally) after the meeting ends. At the end of the day, I'm a numbers guy - statistically speaking, I'm fine with paying $1,000 on steaks and drinks to close a $100,000 deal.

You might think that many of these points are minor concerns, but they quickly add up. If you don't take advantage of the sensory appeal that is within your control, you are putting yourself at a huge disadvantage.

Imagine that two salespeople approach the same client with identical offers. The first salesperson arrives wearing a dirty old sneakers and a wrinkled shirt. The client smells cigarette smoke and bad breath as he meets the salesman's weak handshake. For an hour or so, the client picks at a bland, over-salted plate of food while the salesman shares the details of the proposal in a meek voice.

The next day, the client hears the second offer. This salesman arrives in a tailored suit. His hair is cut and combed in place. He greets the client with a firm handshake, and speaks confidently about the details of his proposal as they enjoy a delicious dinner.

Who do you think ends up closing the deal? Though their offers were identical, their presentations could not have been more different. The businessman who made the effort to appeal to the client's senses has a clear advantage.

Look Good, Feel Good, Do Good

Let's change gears for a second. Thus far we have focused on how your appearance affects the way others perceive you. Now, let's focus on how your appearance affects the way you perceive yourself.

It's important to understand that the minds of every person on earth are filled with garbage. Even the most successful people in the world have unwanted insecurities spiraling through their heads at all times. We tell ourselves we aren't good enough, that nobody cares about our ideas, and that our businesses are doomed to fail.

The Mirror

The Entrepreneurial Evolution

When you take time to clean up your appearance, you also clean out some of these garbage thoughts. When you catch a glimpse of your ironed dress shirt, trimmed beard, and polished shoes in the mirror, you feel good. Your confidence increases. You begin to see yourself as a successful person, and start to behave like one too.

I like to play a game with the people I work with where I ask them to describe what a successful person looks like. Perhaps you'd like to give it a try:

Close your eyes and try to picture a successful person in your mind. What do you see?

I've found that most people give me the same answer. The archetype of success is no secret. The exercise usually evokes images of physically fit individuals who are well-dressed, well-groomed, and brimming with confidence.

Granted, your imagination may come up with some slightly different results depending on what is most important to you. I usually imagine a successful person as somebody who plays sports, since I have learned to value the workplace stamina of athletic people.

Once you get this far with the exercise, I want you to write down every single detail about the person you imagined. How do they look? What do they represent? How do they behave? How is their posture? Write it all down. This is the person I want you to become. This is now your personal end-game; every detail you wrote down is now a goal you've set for yourself.

The Bottom Line

The bottom line is that the mirror can say a lot about your chances of success as a business owner. Neglecting your appearance and your personal presentation puts you at a serious disadvantage, while appealing to your client's senses can give you a serious edge.

The game of sales is all about statistics. Let's assume you start with a 10% chance of success based on your existing knowledge of the product and its benefits. Every lesson you take from this course bolsters your chances. If I had to assign a number value this section, I would say that the lessons here will up your chances by at least 15%. If I told you a steak, a shower, and a haircut could increase your sales success by 15%, wouldn't you give it a shot?

I encourage you to share this with your employees. Try my exercise and apply its lessons. I promise that you will see an increase in your closing rates, as well as a noticeable boost to your employees' self-esteem.

Chapter 11:
Too Good to Be True

Boxing, business, and bass fishing have more in common than you might think. In all three, survival depends on one's ability to identify traps and walk away from something that looks too good to be true.

For both the counter-puncher and the fisherman, deception is the name of the game. All kinds of rigs and techniques have been thought up to increase the chances that mistakes get made. Like an angler floating bait into a creek mouth, veteran boxers will leave false openings for their opponents using a technique known as "drawing." Charging straight ahead in a fight is too risky; rather than rushing forward, great fighters force their opponents to overcommit. When drawing, the boxer creates a deliberate defensive gap to tempt the opponent to punch. Their opponent sees a juicy opportunity when the hand drops or the head dips forward, when really a sharp counter-hook is waiting for them. Success depends on exploiting their opponent's mistakes.

I have personally been on both sides of the fishing line.

There will be many times in your business and family life that an amazing deal or once-in-a-lifetime opportunity presents itself to you. It will be as tempting as a free punch or an easy meal.

In these situations, remember that your survival depends on your ability to recognize threats. In boxing, bass fishing, and business, we must remember the old saying that "if it looks too good to be true, it probably is."

There are people out there whose goal is to deceive and exploit you - I know this because I'm one of those people.

The Baiting Business

I am a Certified Hacker. I work with financial institutions who contract me to lie to their workers and exploit their security systems. In doing so, I show them where they're vulnerable to malicious hackers, and the company patches up any holes before real damage is done.

Interestingly, I found that the easiest way to breach high-security institutions was through basic social engineering. Dangling the right bait in front of trusting people can get you far. Let me share a story to keep you from falling victim to the kind of game I played:

7 years ago, my team and I accepted a contract to hack into the servers of a high-security institution. We knew their security was strong the minute we starting probing for weaknesses. We hit digital dead-ends everywhere we turned. Weeks of work got us nowhere. My team filled hard-drives with gigs of reconnaissance and testing data with no real solution in sight. Security on this client's server was too tight - their system could not be breached.

Instead of giving up, I took charge of the project. The company's security couldn't be breached, so I turned to any organization's weak point: people. I decided to create a Trojan virus; once activated, it would give me backdoor access to the computer system. Now, I just had to lure someone into my trap.

I uploaded the virus to a USB key, and started to think about my bait. Bass are drawn to shimmering, juicy-looking jigs; boxers commit to big punches when they spot drooping hands or flared elbows. My lure had to be subtle, but irresistible.

Before I continue with this story, the amount of effort I put into this deception needs to be acknowledged. I spent a considerable amount of time and effort putting this scheme together. I scouted out the facility in person and combed their virtual security systems. I thought about how their employees thought, and developed a rough understanding of their work schedules. If this all seems excessive to you, then you're exactly the kind of person that needs this lesson. Realize that what I did is neither rare nor exceptional. Scam-artists like me are out there right now, innumerable, dreaming up bigger schemes with badder intentions than I could ever imagine. Keep this in mind as you move forward with your business.

I labeled the USB "Financial and Salaries 2009," and drove to the company offices. From where I sat in my car, my plan seemed hopeless. The building looked as impregnable in real life as it was in the virtual world. My view of the front entrance was filtered through the links of a heavy-duty security fence. A guard was posted nearby, and nobody was allowed near the gates without proper identification.

I watched and waited until I saw a green Ford Crown Victoria roll into the employee parking lot. I timed my move carefully so that I could reach the driver before he was too close to the guard. I grabbed my bait, jumped out of the car, and jogged lightly up behind the employee as he began making his way to the gate.

"Sir, I think this fell out of your bag!" The man was gracious, even though he was in a hurry. He took the USB key and carried on.

I walked back to my car, opened my laptop, and waited for the incoming connection. The trap was set. I assumed that every employee would want to see their firm's salary numbers, and that if this man did not snoop, he would at least pass it along to somebody who would. You'd have to be stupid to pass up that opportunity, right?

Thirty minutes later, an employee activated the file,

and I gained full control of their computer. From there, my team tore down their server security with the kind of enthusiasm you might expect after weeks of being denied. The network went down, and our contract was fulfilled. All it took was some juicy bait, and I was able to trick this employee into helping me reach my goals.

Just like the baited fish and prizefighter, this security firm would have been safe if they understood that some things are too good to be true. There are con artists out there who make their money scamming honest people. Being aware of these threats increases your chances of survival, like the fish who knows about fishermen, and the boxer who knows about counter-punching.

The business world is full of deceptive people. Scams are everywhere - you can find them in your junk mail folder every day. Of course, junk mail is amateur stuff; it lacks subtlety and promises too much to be believable. A boxer who throws his arms up and gifts you his chin is not fooling anybody. The fighter who knows exactly what he's doing when he seems to be making a mistake is the real threat. Real scam "artists" earn their namesake.

People will come to you with amazing offers, so good you can't refuse. They will be believable, difficult to pass up, and usually available for a limited time only. If a salesman pitches to you with any hint of pressure or urgency, it's almost certainly a scam. You should consider any mention of the dealer being "sold out with one final spot available," or this being the "last day to get this deal" to be a serious red flag.

Some scam-artists are even more sophisticated. They may assemble a task force hired to profile you. The information they gather is then used to craft your dream deal. It will be the most amazing offer you have ever heard.

In these cases, the best thing you can do is remove yourself from the equation entirely. Consult other professionals, bringing the offer by at least two people with informed opinions and experience on the matter. See if you are still interested afterwards. Your risk will be greatly reduced if you get two objective endorsements.

Imagine how boring boxing would be if a fighter could consult two trainers before every move they made. Nobody would ever get exploited, and nobody would bother watching.

No Freebies

You're not the only one in the business equation who's going to be wary of "incredible offers." Even if you have the best intentions, offering something that seems "too good to be true" will put your prospects on guard. If you want to craft a truly compelling offer, you need to be sensitive to this perception.

A number of years ago, I sat in on a meeting with a prominent sports marketing company. They wanted to drive subscriptions to their website by giving users a chance to win free Super Bowl tickets.

After a few weeks of advertising, they drew 100 winning names from their user database. The customer relations staff sat down to make the calls informing the winners of their prizes, looking forward to a day of screaming celebrations and excited energy.

But when they tried to contact the winners, the sports marketing reps kept getting hung up on! The winners treated these bringers of big news like inconsiderate telemarketers. The deflated customer relations crew were laughed at, sworn at, and told "not to call this number again." The team later told me that giving away those Super Bowl tickets was the hardest part of their campaign. Their offer seemed too good to be true, so nobody took it seriously.

Keep this guarded mentality in mind as you put together your own promotions. If you're trying to base your marketing on "freebies," you'll get sub-par results. Prospects will suspect a hidden agenda and lump you in with the scammers of your industry. Sweetening the deal with an add-on is one thing, but unsolicited freebies are always highly suspect. Once you internalize this idea, your approach to marketing will evolve, and you'll be less prone to overselling your product or service.

The Bottom Line

Too Good to be True

If something looks too good to be true, it probably is. In my experience, 1 out of every 1,000 "incredible offers" is legitimate, and as a numbers guy, I don't like those odds.

Be smart – make a habit of turning down amazing offers. Exploiters are everywhere, and a single bad decision can ruin your business. Run any questionable offers by at least two other professionals with no attachment to the situation. If you get two objective endorsements, you may proceed.

Remember - you're not the only one who's being wary of incredible offers. Your prospects will not respond well to freebies and "unbelievable opportunities," even when you offer them with the best intentions. Be careful not to put prospects on guard with your promotions.

Chapter 12:
Breadcrumbs on the Table

Bruce Lee spoke once about not fearing the man who had practiced 10,000 kicks one time, but rather he who had practiced one kick 10,000 times. Early in my martial arts training, I was made to understand the wisdom behind these words.

During my competitive Karate career, my father told me to choose one kick that I would practice 1,000 times each week. I didn't understand why at the time; I thought I was limiting my development in some way by ignoring advanced techniques. But I did it anyways. I chose to work on my roundhouse kick, the mawashi geri.

After a few months of dedicated practice, my kick got better. I focused on little things, like rolling my hips, and keeping the knee of my kicking leg horizontal to the floor. Week by week and kick by kick, these little adjustments started adding up.

Eventually, mawashi geri became my strongest weapon. It developed more power, speed, and accuracy than anything else in my arsenal, and became responsible for most of my wins.

I came to understand why my father had insisted I focus on a single technique. Victory came not when I tried to expand my arsenal, but when I took time to refine it.

The lesson stuck with me, and has greatly impacted the way I build businesses today. It doesn't matter whether we're talking about business, family, or martial arts, there's always work to be done on the basics, and doing that work always pays off.

Breadcrumbs on the Table

I've noticed one consistent mistake being made by the business owners who hire me as a consultant. It's the same mistake I made as a young *karateka*; they try to add to their arsenal, rather than refining their existing techniques. In their eagerness to expand the company, they fail to address the flaws in their current system. Call center, customer service, and sales department processes are never perfected, and this persistent room for improvement means that sales are lost every day.

Though losing the occasional sale may seem inconsequential at first, it's not. When you're fighting for survival, every little bit counts. I refer to these lost sales as "breadcrumbs" because they're easily overlooked, and they feed your business in exactly the same way as this leftover food item; eating a few won't satisfy you, but they can fill you up if you get a lot. Ignore these precious morsels, and your business might just starve.

The trouble starts when business owners spend money on expansion without getting their ducks in a row at the sales and customer service level. There's still sales revenue to collect, but they decide to spend money on marketing instead. It makes no sense; they could make more money with less effort by closing the deals their unrefined process turns away. They're ordering more food when there are still many breadcrumbs left on the table.

Choosing to expand your business before you've refined your process can cost your business 30-50% in sales as the breadcrumbs go to waste.

Fortunately, you can reclaim that 30-50% if you're willing to refine your basics. There are easy and actionable changes you can make to your business that will produce amazing results. You just need to understand the problem and make the proper adjustments before trouble strikes.

Once your business reaches the point where you're considering spending more money on marketing, stop and examine your sales, call center, and customer service processes. Make sure you're not leaving any money behind before you go spending more. Small tweaks can make a big impact on your revenue, and this is where I can help you most.

I recently helped a business boost their revenue by 53.5% after 6 months of process refinement and "breadcrumb collection." A few tweaks to their phone system, internal communications, and customer service process was all it took. No increase to their marketing budget was required.

Take a look at the approach we used, and imagine the revenue these changes could generate for your business:

Phone System and Sales Calls

1. Customers on hold were previously forced to listen to boring "muzak" while they waited to speak with an agent. We substituted bland background music for a script narrating why the client should work with us, explaining our value and otherwise bringing attention to our main selling points. This one change dropped the call abandon rate from 65% to 30%. Unsurprisingly, people found relevant information more engaging than muzak. While the prospects waited and listened, their interest in our company would build. Quite often, they were sold on the product before our agent had even answered the call.

2. Some customers were getting upset by poor phone connections. There was a positive correlation between the number of low-quality calls and hang-ups. We took action and upgraded the VOIP phone system to a high-performance PBX. This simple change decreased the number of hang-ups significantly, and increased the average call length by 15%.

3. We developed a thorough sales script for receptionists that put contingencies in place to counter common client objections. This gave every receptionist the tools to handle hard questions and customer complaints. This sales script adjustment boosted sales performances at all levels. Over-the-phone sales increased by 27.5%.

It's important to understand the nature of the script we used so that its value can truly be understood. Your receptionist should not be railroaded by your script. You can expect the deal to fall apart any time your sales agent starts reading verbatim from a screen. Instead of a rigid speech, have the script offer guidelines for different scenarios. It should suggest general courses of action for the receptionists to follow, rather than put words in their mouths.

For example, the script might read: "Would the client like to proceed and place their order?" If yes, then the agent would begin providing order instructions in a natural, conversational way. If no, the script will simply say: "Offer the client a 20% discount." Crucially, the script does not include a robotic pitch for the agent to read. The agent can work this discount offer into the call naturally, rather than intoning corporate copy.

Compare this conversational approach to the common alternative that I see. The customer says no, and the agent drones through their sales script for the twentieth time that afternoon. "Sir, we are sorry to hear that you have decided not to proceed with this order. Because you are a valued customer, we would like to offer you a 20% discount. Is this agreeable to you, sir or madame?"

The difference is night and day. Reading off of a script

or screen is a poor way to approach a sale. Nobody wants to feel like they're interacting with a machine, and that's exactly what happens when you give your receptionist a rigid script.

4. In addition to providing a script, we gave all sales reps single-click access to a huge information center that contained everything we knew about our products and services. When we reviewed our salespeople's performances through an objective lens, we found that they were able to answer customers questions in a satisfactory way about 70% of the time. However, some of the junior reps struggled with that final 30%. These were tough questions about refunds, grandfathered accounts, and so on. By giving our sales staff one-click access to our complete information database, we increased our customer satisfaction to over 90%. We recovered a number of dead deals, and watched the confidence of our new hirees grow as a result.

5. When you're trying to refine your basics, remember that there's nothing more fundamental than fear. We took time to address the insecurities that our sales agents were harbouring. We had 32 sales reps on our staff roster, and found that every single one had some kind of sales-related anxiety that was affecting their ability to close deals. Some were afraid of being assertive, while others feared angry feedback from customers. We discussed these fears openly, and tried to find solutions where we could. Many managers are content to tell their employees: "Hey, don't be afraid. Think about the call as a game." We weren't. Instead, we sat each person down and made an effort to address the unique fears they experienced. Giving our employees a chance to vent and offering whatever support we could had dramatic results. Sick days and vacation time dropped down, office morale improved, and closing rates started to climb.

Internal Communications and Structure

1. Employees were losing productivity with inefficient internal communication. Previously, they were visiting each other's desks to ask questions. This meant a lot of unproductive time spent walking back and forth.

   We eliminated this wastage, restricting all communication between employees to the company's internal chat system. Though it appeared to save only a few seconds worth of "travel time" around the office, the results were impressive.

2. Daily meetings were added to the company process. These meetings ran about 5 minutes in total. Each employee would say a few words about the tasks they planned to finish that day, and the manager logged these tasks to monitor their status. These meetings increased employee accountability, and gave everyone a forum to present problems directly to management. The quality and consistency of employee output improved, and management was able to identify and address issues faster than ever.

3. Some employees were struggling with task management. They would blitz through the easy work early in the month, avoiding the tough tasks for as long as possible. This caused a number of internal delays. To eliminate this problem, we implemented a simple task system that every employee would be required to work with. Managers scheduled tasks each month, and employees had to structure their work day based on assigned "priority levels." We held weekly meetings, and began each with a review of tasks, priority status, and questions or concerns. This simple system stopped employees from avoiding the hard work, and productivity increased.

Customer Service:

1. Customer service calls were frequently being received by members of the sales team. The salespeople at this business were all very nice, and took time out of their day to help customer who called in, which was a problem. Customer service is important, but it's not what we pay our sales team for. Not only was this wasting expensive sales resources, but it meant that customers were getting sub-par service, since our salespeople were not trained for this task.

   To address this problem, we instructed our sales team to transfer callers to a customer service representative any time the conversation veered in that direction. This freed up the sales lines for selling, and produced better customer service experiences.

2. Bad reviews are a problem for all businesses, and this company was no different. To manage our reputation, we added a review system to the company website, making it easy for customers to express their comments and complaints to us directly. This helped the company in a number of ways. First, it alerted us any time a customer had feedback, which is something you don't get when they post on sites like Yelp. This let us respond right away, giving us the best chance to recover sales and secure repeat business. As time passed, new visitors to the website would see these positive, professional interactions, and word of our quality customer service spread. Hosting our own reviews also gave us the option to remove negative comments anytime they spiraled out of control. In the end, adding an on-site review system decreased the amount of negative reviews appearing on public websites by about 50%.

3. The company lacked an appropriate "escalation process" to deal with angry clients. Generally speaking, when customers get upset, the first thing they do is demand to talk to the owner or manager. Our reps only had two options: disturb the owner multiple times per day, or refuse and frustrate the client further. To resolve this problem, we assigned one employee the role of "customer service manager." The customer service manager's job was to convert angry callers into happy clients. We invested time and money into training and education, and gave them special authority to dispense discounts and free services when needed. The results were very good - our company's reputation improved, and we recovered many sales.

Once again, minor process refinements paid off. All these little crumbs added together to make for quite the meal; a 53.5% increase in 6 months is astronomical, and the business owner didn't have to increase his marketing budget by a single cent.

The advice prescribed here is specific to that business owner's unique circumstances, but the overarching lesson applies to everyone: little tweaks make a big difference, and breadcrumb count!

I've assembled some more breadcrumb collection tips for you here, but the list of process adjustments you can make is never-ending.

Delegate Stubborn Sales

Learn to delegate sales work properly.

Every entrepreneur will deal with prospects who hum and haw about a purchase. They request meeting after meeting, or light up your email inbox with questions. They're often just wasting your time, and will delay doing business indefinitely.

You can avoid these time-sinks if you delegate properly. When you're assigning tasks to your all-star salespeople, remember that some small deals aren't worth fighting for. Meandering clients can be worth as much as 10-15% of your sales (if they'd ever pull the trigger), but that amount isn't worth wasting your A-team's time. They're supposed to focus on the high-yield targets.

Instead, close these deals using entry-level salespeople, or by creating an automated online process using E-commerce shops, video pitches, and order forms.

The bottom line is that you need to use your strong sellers on big deals. Point your big guns at monsters, not ants!

Emphasize Customer Service

Customer service skills are extremely important, yet criminally underappreciated by many business owners. When I bring up the subject of customer service, they scoff and say: "I prefer to spend my money on sales, not unhappy clients and dead deals." This is the wrong attitude to have, since quality customer care always leads to more sales.

I was raised in a household that emphasized respect, and I bring this focus to my business dealings as well. I make a serious effort to monitor my customer service processes. Doing so lands me more repeat business, and gets me lots of referrals. It also gets my company "indirect referrals" through great reviews, which we know are vital. A single stunning review can boost your business for years as more and more people come across it.

Improving your customer service process will also help you recover dead deals. If your process is attentive and accommodating, you can easily convert an angry customer into a loyal one. The trick is to imagine yourself in their position so that you can offer them what they want. Sometimes it's a simple apology and acceptance of guilt:

"John, after reading your file, I can say one thing for sure - we dropped the ball, and I'm sorry for that. I will do whatever it takes to make it right." Hearing this, many angry customers will lose the desire to argue. They'll be ready to talk instead.

I've had this approach used against me before with great effect. After buying my wife a new Dodge, we noticed a number of mechanical problems that the dealership would need to address. However, each time we went to the Dodge dealership, they seemed unable to locate the issues we had described. It got to a point where we even brought in a video recording as proof, but they still sloughed it off and refused to help us.

Their customer service was appalling, and I was

furious. After a few months of this kind of treatment, I'd had enough. My wife had invested so much of herself into our business, and I just wanted to see her happy.

I went to the dealership pumped up and ready for war. As soon as I arrived, I marched straight into the manager's office and asked him if he was in charge. I was not about to back down.

Though my voice was quiet, the manager felt my energy right away, and he reacted perfectly. "I know we've kept you waiting way too long. Are you going to pound me?" he asked, offering me exactly what I wanted in that moment. Of course, I was not about to attack this man. I felt myself cool off almost immediately as the realization set in.

At this point, we were back to square one. Once again, I started to describe the problems we had been having, and got more of the same. He had enough customer service skill to get me ready to talk, just so he could talk me in circles.

The Dodge was never fixed. We had to sell it for much less than we wanted. It was still a positive experience - a lesson, not a failure; at least I got to see the approach I teach used against me!

Cross-Sell

Your strategy must include cross-selling. This practice involves selling related or complementary products to your customers, and it is one of the most effective methods of marketing. If you have multiple services, then it is worthwhile to promote them to existing clients with whom you already have "face time." In order of difficulty, cross-selling is most effective in person, manageable over the phone, and tough via email. Ideally, you want to meet and spend time with the clients who you're targeting for a cross-sale.

Cross-selling is a great practice, so long as the sales agent or customer service representative goes about it the right way. Here is an example of the wrong approach:

"Hello sir, I see you purchased our large sofa. I can also offer you our small sofa for $199."

This salesperson is definitely cross-selling; the small sofa is a clearly-related product that complements the large sofa very well, and even makes sense as part of a living room set. Still, this is a poor interaction with the client, and will almost certainly not end with a successful sale.

In this case, a little social engineering is just what doctor ordered. Cross-selling is especially effective once you understand how people think. Human beings are naturally very social creatures, and we like to follow the herd. A cross-sale is much more likely to succeed if you present the deal as something other people have already taken advantage of. In the case of our furniture salesman, we see that he did not present the small sofa deal as something that other people found appealing.

Consider the following example, using what we now know about people's tendency to follow the herd:

"I'm happy to see you decided on our large sofa, John. That's a great piece of furniture that gets a lot of positive reviews. Some people prefer the set to keep a consistent theme, so I usually recommend this small sofa. Most of our clients buy these two as a pair anyway to take advantage of the promotion we started last week."

This is a much stronger proposal, and the kind you should use to model your cross-selling strategy.

Build Referral Relationships

Affiliating with other companies is a great strategy when done correctly. You'll read more about this later. Sending your clients to a third party will garner you a percentage of every sale, and all you need to do send an email linking your customer to the vendor. The vendor does the rest while you collect the money.

You will need to have a contract in place that outlines all terms and commissions beforehand.

As a general rule, your affiliates should sell complementary products or services that don't compete with your business in any way.

You must be particular about who you choose to associate with. Know exactly what kind of company you are recommending to your clients. You cannot recommend bad vendors, even in situations where you stand to make serious money. Making the sale won't be worth losing the client.

When used properly, referral agreements are an incredible asset. I've helped many people create businesses that purely referral-based; these socially gifted individuals spend their days closing deals on the golf course. While this life may not be for you, it speaks to the power of referrals. If you can manage 20-30 different referral relationships at once, revenue will always be streaming in from other companies.

Use Low-Pressure Sales Reminders

It's true that some sales cycles begin with the seller chasing a lead, but many businesses go about it the wrong way. I don't believe in pressure sales.

Instead, I incorporate the "3 Reminder Rule" into my sales strategy. If a sales prospect somehow fizzled out or disappeared along the way, I will give the client 3 separate phone/e-mail reminders in hopes of recovering the lead. The first and second messages are basic reminders with incentives to take action, but the third takes a different approach. In the body of this final email, I thank the prospect for their time, express understanding for their decision, and tell them that I look forward to serving them again in the future. This simple follow-up strategy produces great results. By the third reminder, many people end up apologizing for the delay, and move forward with the deal.

Remember that a client who hasn't taken action isn't necessarily disinterested in your product. People just get busy sometimes; they swept up in the rhythm of life, and forget to complete a purchase that they badly wanted to make. This is why the 3-reminder rule is so effective. It's a way to engage your client and rekindle their interest without being pushy. By the third email, you will have created a sense of urgency. The customer realizes that they will not be receiving another reminder in the future, and finally makes the effort to complete their order.

The Bottom Line

The bottom line lesson here is that you cannot rush your business' expansion. Refine your arsenal before you start adding to it. Your process must be polished before you start spending money on marketing. Most businesses focus too much on the big picture when there are basic process improvements to be made, and sales being left behind. It simply does not make sense to spend more money on marketing and expansion to drum up new business when you're leaving 30-50% of your sales on the table.

Make the time to assess your business process, and do it as though you were a stranger hired to be hyper-critical. Objective analysis is key, whether you're trying to build a winner's mentality, or find flaws in your business process. This is the same approach I use to build positive experiences and remove distractions, and it's exactly how the process improvements in this section came to be.

Don't approach this task looking to take action, or you'll quickly find yourself overwhelmed. Instead, document your findings and compile a list of changes you could make. Once the list is ready, find somebody internally who will be able to tackle it, and start small.

Try to implement some of the process refinements I have suggested here. This list is nowhere near complete, but it will get you moving in the right direction. Monitor your numbers – you will be amazed at the results that a little attention to detail can yield.

Chapter 13: Make More Money Without Hiring Employees

Much of my work as a business consultant is about identifying money-making opportunities that my clients miss. Sometimes it's matter of refining a faulty sales process, or tweaking the work environment to increase productivity. Other times, it means expanding the business, approaching untapped markets to take on new projects. This chapter focuses on the latter.

I've worked with more businesses owners than I can count, and I can say without a doubt that most have reservations about expansion. They worry that they lack the time, money, and manpower they need to launch a whole new company branch.

Their concerns are valid: expanding a small business is definitely a gamble, and a costly one at that, but we're really talking about two different things. The expansion they have in mind involves increasing marketing budgets and hiring more employees to access new revenue streams. This isn't what I mean. Spending money to make money is easier said than done, and rushing this kind of expansion is exactly what I warned against in Chapter 12. It's not something I recommend unless conditions are perfect.

When I talk about "expanding business" in this chapter, I mean expanding your opportunities for profit, not the size of your company. While both forms of expansion are meant to tap into new markets and make you money, there are many important differences between the two. Expanding the size of a company is risky, time-consuming, and expensive, whereas expanding your business can be simple, safe, and highly profitable when done properly.

In this chapter, I share a safe and cost-efficient way for entrepreneurs to tap into new markets to make more money, all while avoiding the hassle of hiring. Applying the ideas presented in this section can realistically double your income in a single day's work - I know how ludicrous this sounds, but it's true. Allow me to explain.

Expand Your Business, Don't Expend Your Resources

For the sake of this lesson, imagine that you're a realtor. Your job is to sell houses, but you're also regularly rubbing elbows with people in the home services and renovation industries. It's just the nature of your job; when someone buys a new house, they need duct and carpet cleanings, new countertops, and other related services before they're settled. You see these interactions happen all of the time, and your clients will occasionally ask you for recommendations.

Though you may not to realize it, there is a tremendous opportunity here to expand your business and increase your earnings, so long as you're willing to get a little more involved in your client's life. Anyone in the home service industry would kill for regular access to interested clients so ready. You're in a privileged position where you can help the client and the company, all while making a nice commission.

Unfortunately, most people let these opportunities go to waste simply because they aren't selling what their clients are looking to buy. They think that the only way to profit from this demand is to supply the services themselves, and they lack the resources for that kind of expansion. In our example, you're just one person working in real estate - how in the world are you going to hire, train, and manage a team of duct cleaners and kitchen renovators? Do you think you'll be very profitable after you've paid all of their wages?

There's a way to make it work. You don't need more manpower, and you don't need to spend money. In fact, you don't even need much time.

The Power of Affiliation

I have already spoken briefly about the power of affiliating in Chapter 12. When done properly, affiliating is one of the best ways to expand your business, without expending your resources. There are people out there willing to do the work for you, so long as you're there to feed them clients.

Affiliating is a rare way to make money without spending it. The key is to choose affiliates that complement your business. Their products and services should be a byproduct of your own. For example, if you run a publishing company, you can get your commission by referring clients to cover art designers, marketing firms, or editors. A candy shop can connect with florists and holiday card companies. The list goes on. Your business will almost always part of a larger industry, and it shouldn't be hard to find companies whose services pair well with yours.

Set aside one full work day next month. Pick up your pen and start a list of quality companies whose services complement your own. Search all of their phone numbers online, and write them down.

Once your list is complete, start making calls to arrange meetings. After 8 hours, you'll probably have spoken to 50-60 business owners. You'll encounter a lot of dead-ends, but at the end of the day, will have come up with a list of maybe 10 businesses that are hungry for work and willing to meet.

When you meet with these business owners, explain that you're able to set them up with buyers on a regular basis in exchange for a small commission. Request 5%-10% of the revenue or a fixed fee on all sales that you bring to their company. They're essentially paying a small finder's fee on their sales, which is more appealing than most marketing deals - if you know any marketers who only charge for services that lead to a sale, definitely jump on that offer!

If we go back to the real estate example we used earlier, the value of this affiliate approach quickly adds up. Let's say your average deal gets you a 2.5% commission. This works out to about $20,000 for an average-sized house - a nice profit.

As you're closing the deal, the homeowner mentions that they'll need to hire a moving service. You give them the number of the mover you've partnered with, and instantly make $20 for writing down 10 digits.

Your client says that they want to clean their ducts and carpets so that they have a fresh start in their new home - you share two more phone numbers and earn another $150.

Now, suppose that they are looking for a major renovation. A $70,000 kitchen and bathroom overhaul puts a life-changing $10,500 in your pocket, and at what cost to you? The vendors who wanted the job put in all of the effort. They had to explain their service and finalize the sale. You spent one day populating your contact list, and seconds sharing phone numbers with your clients, and now you have endless opportunities for revenue in new markets. You didn't need to hire anybody or worry about managing new employees; you've greatly expanded your business without expending any resources, aside from one 8-hour work day.

The Bottom Line

Make More Money

"Step outside the box— expand, don't expend!"

Biplov'16

The Entrepreneurial Evolution

The bottom line is that you don't need to hire more employees to make more money. Expand, don't expend.

Affiliates are a powerful tool when used properly, and their application here speaks to my larger philosophy about working around obstacles you encounter in your business career. Remember, if you hit a wall, you don't have to break through it, or climb over top. Sometimes the wall is big and strong, and you'd consume too many resources trying to overcome it. Instead, we avoid this obstacle entirely, gaining access to the revenue streams we wanted without having to face the issue of limited manpower. There is almost always a way to bypass the problem, but you need to think outside the box to find it - after all, who would have thought that 8 hours and a handful of phone numbers could change your life?

Chapter 14:
Employee Appreciation

Treating others as you would like to be treated can take you far in all facets of life. The "golden rule" can do wonders for your personal and professional relationships, and it's the guiding principle I use to manage my employees.

I personally make an effort to treat all people the same way, because I believe all people are the same. We all came from the same place, and one day we'll all go to the same place. Whether you're a paying customer, or the employee who scrubs the urinals clean, you're a person, and I will treat you as I wish to be treated.

I've found that this idea is lost on many modern business owners. Stuck on traditional workplace hierarchies, they march around the office like drill sergeants, convinced that their job is to bully their staff. The only raises around the office are when minimum wage gets bumped up, and benefits are completely off the table. In their minds, all that matters is reducing overhead without impacting the customer's experience; employees are expendable.

Unfortunately, the market supports this way of thinking. Business owners have a huge inventory of people looking for work at all times, which means that they always have the option of shopping around. Why pay an employee $15 per hour when there are thousands of people lining up to perform the same work for $12 per hour? At face value, employers have little incentive to pay competitive wages, or even treat their employees particularly well.

In this section, I hope to show you otherwise. Employees are your most precious assets, and they must be treated this way. Spending a little more now will save you lots in the future.

You Reap What You Sow

Most businesses won't be successful unless their employees feel appreciated. People tend to work harder for people they like; it's just human nature. When your employees like their jobs and feel appreciated around the office, they're more productive. They start to care about their work.

If you're a spiritual person, you understand that "you reap what you sow." In other words, treat your employees well, and they'll reciprocate.

Consider the following example:

Danielle makes minimum wage working at a call center. She works 9-hour shifts from Monday to Friday, including the unpaid half-hour she gets for lunch.

Danielle's boss is nasty. He's the kind of guy who sighs into the receiver when you call in sick to make sure you feel guilty about missing work. He worries constantly about getting his "money's worth" for his employees' wages, and only addresses Danielle to criticize her.

How do you think these work conditions affect Danielle's performance? Do you think she's highly motivated to make calls, close deals, and give the best customer service she can? Is Danielle likely to recommend her boss's company to any of friends or family members? How much energy is she going to give to an unappreciative boss?

Danielle doesn't care, because nobody cares about Danielle. She spends much of her 9-hour work day distracting herself from the work and people she dislikes. She stretches out her bathroom breaks, idles on the line with disinterested customers, and endlessly refreshes her Facebook feed when nobody's watching. She stumbles into work in the morning, bleary-eyed and disconnected. She clocks out the second her shift ends. She never thinks about her job outside of the office, and doesn't have positive things to say when family or friends ask about work. Danielle's job is a necessary evil, a way to pay the bills (barely), and a part of her life she wants to give as little attention as possible.

Employee Appreciation

The Entrepreneurial Evolution

Is Danielle the kind of employee you want working for you?

Across town, Jordyn works in a rival call center. She earns $1 more than minimum wage, and gets paid for her 30-minute lunch break.

Jordyn has a great relationship with her boss, and she's happy with her job. She feels lucky to have found a position that pays a bit more, and gets the sense that her hard work is appreciated around the office. Jordyn's boss is complimentary, supportive, and helpful. She knows she can always come to him with any problems she has at the office.

If Jordyn and Danielle were sitting down for their annual reviews, do you think you'd be able to guess who performed better that year? Who closed more sales? Whose average call time was longer?

Who do you think cost the company more money?

At face value, it looks like Jordyn is the more expensive asset. Jordyn is paid more, and effectively gets another 2.5 hours tacked on to her paycheck each week for her lunch breaks. But there's much more to the picture.

Jordyn is happy, which means she's motivated to perform at her best. She works harder to support a business that's been good to her, thereby generating more income for the owner. Jordyn is more likely to stay with the company, which means less money must be spent for HR to find and train new employees. She'll tell her friends and family about her great job, and encourage them to support a company that takes such good care of its staff.

On the other hand, Danielle is miserable. She doesn't care about you - you're just another capital-B "Boss" who won't give her a break. She is completely unmotivated.

The truth is that Danielle is much more expensive than Jordyn. The sales that Jordyn works hard to bring in more than make up for the $1 wage increase and paid lunch breaks. Danielle costs her company many more times in sales what her employer thinks he's saving in wages.

So how do you make sure you work with the Jordyns of the world instead of the Danielles? Follow the golden rule, and make an effort to show your employees they're appreciated. Consider the job you're offering or the work environment you provide from the employee's perspective, and think of small changes you could make to improve their experience.

If you're having trouble coming to terms with the idea of increasing your employee's wages, maybe some lessons from my fight career will help. In boxing, trainers will tell their fighters it's best to "take one punch to avoid three." Some fighters are so desperate to avoid a punch that they'll throw themselves on the ropes or off-balance to evade it. Though the first punch may miss, they end up leaving themselves in a vulnerable position; their opponent is able to walk them down and land two or three more before they can recover. Instead, good fighters will often hold their ground with a high guard as the first punch comes. Though they absorb the initial impact, they leave themselves many different escape options, should their opponent choose to follow-up. The jab lands, but they now have the room and vision they need to slip the cross, and roll under the hook.

What does this have to do with how you treat your employees? You have to be like the the fighter in this example: take a small hit up front, and on your terms, so you can avoid more serious problems later. If you're struggling to justify the extra effort or expense you need to invest to make your employee feel appreciated, just remember that you're taking one punch to avoid three in the future.

The Bottom Line

The bottom line is that your employees need to feel appreciated, one way or another. This simple reciprocal relationship works wonders. I've had over 10 partnerships and countless employees over the years, and almost everyone I've worked with impressed me with their hard work and dedication. Was I just lucky to have found amazing employees, or was I reaping what I sowed?

If you want to increase your company's productivity, lower its turnover rate, and boost your reputation, just remember the golden rule - treat others as you would like to be treated, and everybody wins.

Chapter 15:
The 80% Done Disease

Every single day, I see business owners succumb to a sickness that could have easily been prevented. Though it goes without saying that businesses fall apart for a wide variety of reasons, there is one consistent mental issue I see hurting entrepreneurs who should be thriving.

I call it the "80% done disease." This problem accounts for a lot of small business mortality, but luckily, it's highly treatable. With the proper understanding and plan of action, you can screen yourself for this defect, and recover any losses you may have already incurred. If the symptoms I describe in this section sound familiar, then I'm excited for you - it means your business is about to seriously improve.

The 80% Done Disease

Though the name might not be familiar, this disease affects more people in the business world than the common cold. The "80% done disease" is a kind of delusion where we treat a project as finished when it is really only 80% done. It's a huge mistake, and I see it happen all the time.

When I start a new project, I'm usually very excited. I set to work with gusto and get a lot done very quickly. Before I know it, my project is almost ready to go live; I'm about 80% of the way there. All I have left to do is add some final touches, which I figure will take me a few more hours at most.

With the finish line in sight, I take my foot off of the gas pedal. The majority of the work is behind me, so I begin to treat the project as though it were already finished. I may not even schedule another dedicated work period, figuring I can wrap things up in my spare time.

Never, ever do this. These kinds of thoughts are symptoms of the "80% done disease," and must be avoided at all costs if your business is going to survive.

The "80% done disease" is an easy trap to fall into because that last 20% is usually tremendously boring. During the first phase of a project, my excitement carries me through the long days. Then the novelty wears off, and all there's left to do is grind through the final stages of research, revision, and fine-tuning. The idea of moving onto something new is much more appealing, and in terms of efficiency, using my excited energy to complete 80% of a fresh project sounds like a better use of my time.

This obviously isn't the case. Your bottom line depends on that final 20%. An airplane that is missing a wing is probably about 80% finished, but it clearly isn't ready to fly. If you try to use it, it won't go well.

You may feel as though you are getting a lot done when you charge through the majority of many different projects at once, but you aren't. In fact, you're getting nothing "done" in the literal sense of the word. Finished products are where your money is made.

Imagine your business as a city trying to expand. You think you're building one beautiful skyscraper after another, but when you go to use them, you realize they're all unfinished frames and scaffolding. You've done all of this work, but have nothing useable to show for it. People can't live in scaffolding, and your business can't thrive off of unfinished projects. A business with 10 products that are 80% finished is one that has done a lot of work, and is generating no money.

I understand that you're probably not building cities or airplanes, though. Some things can operate at 80%, right?

Let's imagine that a business owner wants to launch website for a new product. The design is done, but some details are still missing. Namely, the site lacks high-quality pictures and videos, and the page content is a bit short. Still, it is over 80% complete by this point: the servers, coding, menu layout, map listings, and contact forms all look great, and the business owner is pleased.

From the owner's perspective, the project is already a success. The site is running ahead of schedule, and he wants to use this apparent momentum. It's functional as is; the polish will be added later, when he finds the time to produce videos and write better content. He pushes it to launch so that he can start making sales right away.

Unfortunately, neither the owner's audience nor Google's crawlers will see things quite the same way. A website that is 80% complete is nowhere near ready in the eye of the consumer. Users come to websites for that final 20%. Compelling visuals and video showcases are needed to support a product; without strong content to emphasize selling points and build deficiency for the user, the odds of making a sale are extremely low. Search engines also judge your site based on that final 20%. Short copy or duplicate content used as a placeholder will be flagged by web crawlers, and your search ranking will plummet. Without interesting content and visuals to keep users engaged, your bounce rate will skyrocket, and your site will be penalized. Before long, it will be buried at the bottom of the search listings, where it won't be bringing in any business.

The owner's website doesn't convert, and he deems the project a failure. It's a classic case of the 80% done disease; the site was not unsuccessful, it was incomplete! It doesn't matter whether you're an airplane engineer or an online shoe salesperson; the 80% will bring you down if you're not careful.

My default starting point when called in to consult with businesses that are not meeting their goals is to push them to complete all unfinished projects. I scour the reports, highlight any unfinished areas, and push for that final 20%. When I follow up with reports to see what has changed, the results are usually very good. Those items the business owner dismissed as "finishing touches" or "added polish" were actually critical components, like the "nearly-finished" airplane that was still missing a wing.

The Bottom Line

The bottom line is that you should never treat something that is only 80% finished as complete. This is surprisingly hard to resist, especially with projects like websites that can function in the alpha stage. Remember that finished projects are how your money is made.

Chapter 16: Constructive Criticism in the Workplace

Whether you're trying to correct the behaviour of a fussy child or an under-performing employee, giving constructive criticism is always a challenge. It's compulsory in the business world, though; some things just need to be said if your company is going to succeed.

When you really think about it, criticism ought to have a positive connotation. It's what makes growth and evolution possible for artists, athletes, business people, and employees alike. We learn from our failures, but that's only possible when we're aware of them. Accordingly, criticism shouldn't be thought of as a form of nagging or conflict, but instead as a catalyst for self-improvement.

For many people, giving criticism means wading through headaches and hurt feelings, but it doesn't have to be this way. In this section, I will share the approach I use to criticize my employees in a constructive manner. My method avoids the mess of tension and negativity most people make of these conversations, and will help you get the maximum improvement out of every interaction.

Do Shoot the (Emotional) Messenger

The first rule of workplace criticism is to eliminate emotion from the interaction. There is no worse way to deliver a message than to do so emotionally; feelings get hurt, and the point gets lost.

You should never try to criticize an employee when you're angry. Most business owners identify as action takers, and want to call employees on their mistakes as soon as they happen, but this is a mistake. Being a man or woman of action is admirable, but only when you're making the right move. Calling an employee into your office to criticize their work while you're still seething about the mistake they made is always a terrible idea.

Remember to aim before you shoot. Think hard about your intentions: do you want to blow off steam, or improve your company? If your criticism is about emotional release rather than workplace results, you're better off keeping it yourself.

When you want results, you must present your criticism in a way that makes your employee (or family member) receptive to the change you are proposing.

Imagine that you're an employee who just missed an important meeting. As soon as the meeting ends, your boss comes storming out of the board room towards your desk. His eyes are wide and his jaw is set. Before you have even said hello, you're being screamed at. Heads are turning around the office as your boss lambasts you for your mistake. He's working himself up, demanding to know what he's paying you for, and spending most of the "conversation" telling you how badly you've screwed up.

This criticism obviously is not constructive. As the employee in this scenario, you become defensive right away. If you don't shut down entirely, you'll probably get angry as the verbal abuse keeps piling on. Now you're two angry people stuck in an argument; angry people don't care about solving problems, they care about being right.

Would you learn anything from this interaction with your boss? You'd definitely learn how your boss acts when angry, but not much else. Whatever point they were trying to make gets lost in all of the shouting, and you're too busy defending yourself to really hear what's being said. You're not very willing to listen or compromise when you're locked in "fight or flight" mode, and nothing gets resolved.

Play With Delays and Hide Your Hand

Let's reimagine this same scenario, but this time your boss has followed the first rule of offering criticism in the workplace, and remains in control of his emotions.

You realize that you have missed a very important meeting, but you haven't been attacked over it. Instead, your boss sends you a neutral email notifying you that he would like to meet to discuss your absence.

Though you might not realize it at the time, your boss is making a calculated move.

Delaying the conversation serves him in two ways. First, it gives him time to cool off so that an ugly confrontation can be avoided. Secondly, since nobody is attacking you, you're left with plenty of time to think about the mistake you made.

Any time an employer comes raging out of their office to pick a fight, they give their employee the luxury of self-defense. Rather than taking accountability for your mistake, you can think about how unprofessionally your boss is acting.

In contrast, when your employer gives you space and respect, this luxury disappears. There are no longer two guilty parties involved in this interaction. You made a mistake, and you'll be thinking about it for the rest of the day. You reread the email and wonder how the conversation will go. The anticipation eats away at you, along with the guilt. Your boss hasn't said a word, but by using my method of delayed conversation, their message is already being sent.

My approach is effective in part because human beings have an inherent fear of the unknown. Referring back to the previous scenario, you're pretty sure that your boss won't take a swing at you or do anything rash, but that won't stop you from pouring over the worst possibilities in your mind.

The angry alternative approach is less effective for the same reason. When your boss comes raging out of the board room to scream in your face, he shows all his cards at once. While unpleasant, his reaction isn't nearly as terrible as what you imagined. Once you have already experienced the worst, angriest version of your boss, the fear of the unknown dissolves. The employee isn't as afraid of the repercussions anymore, and may be more willing to break the rules again in the future.

As the business owner, staying calm and delaying the conversation is the way to go: your cards remain hidden, leaving you in a powerful position with the unknown on your side.

Attack the Issue, Not Each Other

As you read in Chapter 9, my philosophy emphasizes communication, cooperative action, and working around obstacles. Keep this in mind as we continue with our previous example of the missed meeting.

The hour arrives, and the meeting with your boss finally happens. You're pleasantly surprised; rather than trying to scold you, your boss only wants to make sure it doesn't happen again. You feel lucky to have such a level-headed employer, and now you're willing to listen. You attack the issue together instead of attacking each other, and can now find a permanent solution to the problem.

As your conversation unfolds, it comes to light that you hadn't been scheduling events properly in your Google calendar. It turns out that this why you missed the meeting. It's an easy fix; your boss takes five minutes to run you through a Google calendar tutorial, and you return to your desk with a smile. Your boss's criticism was positive and constructive, and now you're better at your job. You'll never miss another meeting due to a scheduling fumble, and it feels great.

Back in his office, the employer feels great, too. He permanently corrected a small issue that had been causing a big problem for his business, and did so in a way that made everyone very happy.

Model your approach based on the employer in this example. The employee learned a valuable lesson, and no feelings were hurt. Both parties accomplished something, and their work relationship improved.

This outcome isn't possible unless you work together. Your employee can help or hinder your goals - I leave it up to you.

Criticizing the Uncooperative

There will be cases where the recipient of your criticism is unwilling to cooperate. I've worked with many such people; helpful criticism rolls off of them like water off a duck's back. I generally consider this a serious red flag for our future together, but I give most people the benefit of a three-strike rule.

The first warning should be gentle. Deal with the issue as though the vendor or employee made an honest mistake. Assume they're willing to improve.

The second warning must be firmer. Let them know that if their behaviour doesn't change, the third warning will be their last.

On their third strike, they're out. Explain to them that their repeat offences mean one of two things: either they don't care about your business, or they're simply a bad fit. In either case, you don't want this person around you, and they'll need to be released.

This three-strike approach won't always work, of course. If your employee is fulfilling a sensitive role in the business, has a special agreement with you, or is a partner, then you will need to handle things differently. In these circumstances, imagine yourself as a consultant, and take the advice you'd give yourself as an objective observer. For me, this means:

1. Removing any emotion from the interaction as usual. "Do shoot the emotional messenger."

2. Identifying where you have leverage over the other party.

3. Building an incentive for their cooperation. Identify what's important to the other party, and use it to motivate them to perform.

    This method will give you total control.

    When you relax and remove emotion from the interaction, you embrace the kind of cold analysis that I use as the cornerstone of my business philosophy.

When you identify your leverage, you gain power. If you're a client and your vendor is giving you problems, identify whether or not you're a key customer. If you are, either renegotiate the deal, or threaten to take your business elsewhere.

If you have to create incentive, you need to know what's important to the other party. In a business context, it's usually money. I use a "bonus carrot" system with vendors for this reason. I offer a 5% bonus to vendors who deliver quality goods or services on time, and negotiate a penalty system for flagged vendors who I suspect will give me trouble.

The Bottom Line

The bottom line is that there is a right and wrong way to criticize an employee.

Do not act out of anger - it's useless. Criticizing your employee while still bothered by the mistake they made is a fast track to failure. Their performance will not improve, and your relationship will suffer. Instead, play with delays, and keep your cards close to the chest. It will allow you to cool off, think objectively, and give your employee time to take ownership of their mistake.

No one approach will work in every situation, but my overall philosophy is highly adaptable. Communication, cooperation, and cold, objective analysis combine to give you a powerful problem-solving strategy under any circumstances. Try the methods I outlined here, and I promise that you'll have great results.

Chapter 17:
Keep Out of Court

The legal system is complex, and learning how it works is usually not a top priority for an entrepreneur trying to make ends meet.

Unfortunately, you'll probably have some unwanted encounters with the courts at some point in your career. Contracts are part of many business owners' daily processes, and issues with licensing and copyright flare up more than you'd think.

Know what you're getting yourself into. I've seen too many people surprised by the realities of the legal system, and bled dry because of it. They get dragged into a war of attrition on a foreign battlefield, and the only winners are the courts and lawyers involved.

This section will shed some light on the reality of the legal system, and alert you to the risks you take every time you go to court.

A Broken System

Our "system of justice" is fundamentally flawed. When you're called to court, you're not stepping into some romantic arena of justice - you're being led into a business interaction.

Let's imagine that you have a client suing you for $100,000. What's the first thing you do?

After you're done complaining about the situation to all of your sympathetic friends, you decide to consult a lawyer. It seems like the right thing to do; they know the law, and they even offered you a free consultation.

Consulting a lawyer is the default move for most people when they receive news of a pending lawsuit, and it's not wrong. But you can't rely solely on their advice. You're essentially asking a business owner whether or not you should buy their product. Lawyers make money when they're hired to go to court - this is the system that we have in place. Knowing this, what are the chances that your lawyer will tell you that court is a waste of time?

It's not in your lawyer's best interest to advise you to settle, even when it can potentially save you thousands of dollars and years of stress. Imagine that doctors made their money strictly by dispensing medication: what do you think the breakdown of pills prescribed versus healthy lifestyle advice would be for patients with high blood pressure? The pharmaceutical industry would make billions more than it is already, people would be as sickly as ever, and nobody could blame the doctors for it. Everyone has bills to pay; don't hate the player, hate the game.

The legal system is supposed to work differently. Ideally, we would have two divisions of lawyer: the consultants, and the "infantry." The "infantry" would work very much like the public defenders of today, called in to fight on the front line at court once the decision to pursue legal action has already been made. Meanwhile, the consultants would be an entirely separate branch that has no financial stake in whether or not you take your case to trial. You pay the consultants for honest advice, not their time in court.

Our current system has the same people in charge of both your consultation and court battle. It's a major conflict of interests, and it can affect your representative's ability to make an honest call. What do you think your lawyer does when forced to choose between your best interests, and paying his mortgage on time? I think I know the answer.

Still, you're going to need a lawyer at some point, and when you start looking for one, you'll need to be very discerning. In my experience, for every ethical lawyer out there, there's one looking to exploit vulnerable clients. Most people who seek legal counsel are afraid, pressed for time, or unfamiliar with the law, which makes them an easy mark.

Don't settle for the most convenient choice or the person telling you what you want to hear. It took me years to find a lawyer who cared more about giving good advice than about paying his mortgage. I promise that there are amazing lawyers out there, and that you won't regret putting in the effort to find them.

Keep Out of Court

I've had a number of experiences with the court system in my life. Every single one was a waste of effort, even when I had all the cards in my hand. In every single case, I lost money, sleep, and time.

Let me give you an example. I think this experience demonstrates the ineffectiveness of the legal system:

10 years ago, I was a partner at a prominent Israeli advertising firm called the Pirsumedia Group. We had a strong reputation, an innovative website, and hundreds of high-profile customers. When our competitors wondered about "best practices" for their online presence, they looked to our website - it was that good.

Some of our competitors ended up looking a little too closely. We caught one such company who had had blatantly copied our website. It was shameless; the content was verbatim, the interface and images (with copyright!) were identical, and all of our client information had been ported over. It was as if they had copy-and-pasted our website into a template, then given it a new name.

Obviously, we had to take action. The local copyright laws supported us, and stated that there was no need to prove damages in the event that someone has stolen your intellectual property. We consulted with lawyers who reassured us that this was a clear-cut case, and decided to file a lawsuit. We anticipated swift justice and a multi-million dollar payment once the verdict had arrived.

Justice was not swift. 7 years and countless court appearances later, we finally earned a judgment in our favour. We were pleased with a tough win after a long fight, but our celebration was premature. Once the dust had settled, our competitor owed us only a fraction of what we had been promised. Worse still, the losing side successfully appealed the judge's decision, cutting the $250,000 they owed us in half.

Ultimately, the laws were upheld, but justice was not served. The settlement covered our taxes, lawyer's fees, and court expenses, but we didn't see a dime. The legal system enjoyed a fruitful transaction, and we were left with nothing.

But what if a client refuses to pay? Your business won't go anywhere if people can rip you off with no consequences. When this happened to me, court seemed like my only option. I believe in justice, so I tried to seek it out. It wouldn't be the first time I failed.

If you insist on suing a client who has refused to pay, this is what you should expect:

1. Getting started takes longer than you think. The system takes time. Don't get frustrated when it takes you longer than expected to file the necessary paperwork or find an opening in the court office hours.

2. Serving the other party with papers will not be pleasant. In fact, it's kind of a nightmare. You'll either have to do it yourself, or hire an expensive specialty company.

3. You'll probably be asked to settle. This can be a good or bad thing. Typically, settling means that you're sacrificing money for speed. You'll end up with less than half of what you're owed, but at least you'll be able to walk away from a grueling court battle. The guilty party will usually push for this option.

4. If a settlement cannot be reached, it's time to go to court. Now, the real fun begins - or rather, the waiting game continues. It's common to arrive at 9:00AM and wait around all day, only to be told you have to reschedule.

5. It's highly unlikely that your case will be resolved with a single court appearance. Expect to be called in more than once. Every day in court will hurt your productivity, as you eat up work hours and lose focus on business matters.

6. You probably won't be happy with the verdict.

Even when a client refuses to pay, I recommend keeping out of court. It's going to hurt your ego to take the hit without swinging back, but try to think of it as an important lesson. Build a positive experience out of a negative situation.

One objective look at the loss will show that you need to tighten up some part of your process. Evaluate the situation and see where you went wrong, and how you can prevent it in the future. You can usually avoid these kinds of scams if you implement a milestone payment system. Be smart, and try your best to identify quality customers in the future.

Prevention isn't always possible, of course, but a lawsuit is still rarely worth pursuing. Our flawed system does not support justice. Let me give you one final example:

Jeff just bought a $1,000 fridge from Daniel, a salesman at the local appliance center. Once Jeff receives the fridge, he calls his credit card company and claims the transaction is fraudulent. The credit card company does a shallow investigation, and since the appliance company hasn't kept adequate paperwork to verify the sale, the investigator sides with Jeff. The credit card company ends up refunding Jeff's $1,000, and Daniel loses his commision for this "fraudulent" transaction.

In Daniel's mind, he has no choice but to sue Jeff. He needs that commission to get by. Unfortunately, he'll end up spending 1-2 years in court before a verdict is reached. After a prolonged fight, Daniel probably won't get what he deserves. He might get a partial amount, and he might walk away with nothing at all.

Why should Daniel have to wait years before he gets what he's owed in the first place? It's a relatively open-and-shut case, but Jeff will never be treated like the thief he is. This is the system we're stuck with.

I have one final piece of advice to help keep you out of the courts - tie up all loose ends! Agreements need to be formalized in writing if you want to stay out of trouble. This is a great time to involve that reputable lawyer you tracked down. Mistrust, miscommunication, and mistakes lurk in the "grey area" outside of a contract. Cover all of your bases, and leave no maybes. This simple mantra has kept me out of court ever since I learned that it was no place for me.

Courtrooms across the world all look and operate quite differently, but there seems to be one constant: having a legally-sound case does not guarantee that you'll receive your due. Going to trial is always a roll of the dice, and usually a waste of time.

The Bottom Line

The bottom-line lesson here is that you should avoid the court systems whenever possible. Try to reach a settlement if you can. It's almost always preferable to gambling in court.

We are part of a broken system. Having the same person fulfill the role of legal consultant and courtroom representative is a conflict of interest. The majority of lawyers are good, honest professionals, but there are some bad apples out there, and it only takes one to bring you down.

Know the nature of the system you're entering into before you attempt to file a lawsuit. When you sit down with a lawyer, you're asking a business person whether or not you should buy their service. Dishonest lawyers will never advise you to settle, as it's not in their best interest.

Keep out of court. Most of my experiences have been bad. Do whatever you can to avoid it. Try to reach a settlement, put everything you can in writing, keep receipts, and consider adopting a milestone payment structure as needed.

Chapter 18: Measurable Marketing

Marketing is vital to the success of any business. Hard work is important, but marketing is the key to monetization, and yours must be optimized if you want to increase your bottom line.

As you'll read about sales, the topic of marketing cannot be reduced to a single book. This chapter won't transform a marketing novice into a master. Instead, I want to tackle some persistent mistakes that business owners make with their advertising campaigns.

For some reason, business owners in 2016 are still not treating marketing as a measurable expense. It's a huge problem. We have the technology to measure our steps, sleep, and calories, but for some reason, we still ignore important money metrics that pertain to our business. This one mistake sours many entrepreneurs on advertising; they watch their budget burn up with no noticeable effect on sales while the marketing companies continue to thrive.

Blind Branding

In my opinion, the main problem business owners have stems from a flawed understanding of what marketing really is. I first had the value of marketing explained to like this:

The CEO of Coca Cola is flying across the country in his private jet. During a lull in the flight, he wanders into the cockpit and strikes up a conversation with the pilot.

At one point, the pilot turns to the CEO and asks why he spends so much money on advertising.

"I've even seen pictures of Coke billboards in Africa!" the pilot exclaims over the thrum of the engine. "I just don't understand why you're spending millions every year on advertising when you're already the number-one company in the world. Why not just stop already?"

The CEO smiles and jerks his thumb in the direction of the wing. "Why not just stop it already?" he replies, referring to the plane's engines.

The pilot laughs. "I can't turn the engine off - the plane needs it to stay in flight."

The CEO nods. "Exactly."

This is a great story that really underlines the importance of marketing. Unfortunately, its lesson is dated by about 20 years, and it doesn't apply to small businesses.

What the CEO is doing with his African billboards and multi-million dollar campaign is called "branding." You pay money to "get your name out there." Coca Cola-style branding is a game that only huge companies with enormous budgets can play. It's a blind investment without any way to measure its direct impact on sales.

Spending your marketing budget on branding will get your business nowhere. Let's assume that we're working with an annual marketing budget of $10,000. This is a typical amount for small to medium-sized businesses. When you divide this budget up month by month, you're left with about $833. This isn't a lot of money, and it must be managed very strictly if you're going to see results. In these circumstances, branding isn't the way to go. Maximizing the cost-efficiency of your marketing campaign requires strong data, thorough analysis, and constant strategic adjustments, none of which are possible with broad-scale branding.

Even if you spent that entire $833 trying to get your name out there, you'd see zero return. That amount doesn't even qualify as a "shoestring budget" in the branding world. Do you really think you're going to get much air time or billboard space when the big fish in your industry are offering the same advertisers millions? Even a $100,000 budget isn't going to make an impact.

Even worse, your branding will yield no useful data. Consequently, you'll have no idea where you went wrong, and won't have any clue what adjustments need to be made to get results. Your branding investment was made on blind faith the first time around, and it got you nothing. Now, you're in the exact same position you started in, only $833 poorer.

Marketing You Can Measure

Blind branding makes no sense for small business owners operating with modest budgets. Instead, I recommend investing your money into a form of marketing that has measurable results. Quality data is crucial if you want to optimize your budget, and you can measure any marketing asset with a little forethought.

Let's say that you decide to go with pay-per-click (PPC) advertising through Google Adwords. To measure your results, you simply have to assign a different phone number to the ads run in your PPC campaign. This allows you to track all prospects that were directed to your company by your PPC ads. If you want to avoid the hassle of switching phones, you can set your PPC number up so that all calls are forwarded to your existing number. At the end of the month, you'll have concrete data that you can use to gauge the effectiveness of your marketing asset. If your PPC calls are low, you may want to adjust your ad content, or explore different assets altogether.

You can also track the performance of multiple ads at once. For example, a dentist may run different campaigns to promote root canals, filling, implants, and Invisalign braces, and want to know how each distinct ads performs. All she has to do is assign a separate phone number to each. By the end of the year, she'll know how many people called for each treatment, and have a clear idea of how her marketing plan can improve. High-performing ads will be left alone or even scaled back, while the low-performers are tweaked or redone.

Calls can also be recorded to provide you with even more strategic information. Sometimes basic data showing the number of leads and prospects an ad generates doesn't tell the whole story.

I did the online marketing for a client in the business education industry who used call recording to avoid a huge loss. One day, he approached me and said that he wanted to suspend his online campaign. When I asked why, he told me that he had been experimenting with a radio campaign that was generating an unprecedented amount of leds. I was happy for him. I deactivated his account right away.

Fortunately, he took what I said about measuring your marketing effort to heart.

After some time, the client contacted me and asked to reactivate his account. When I asked why, he explained to me how monitoring his calls had just saved his company thousands. Apparently, the radio advertising his company put together offered a free USB stick for those who attended the first free trial course. The idea was to attract prospects to one class, blow them away with quality content, and enlist as many as possible for the second paid course. The response was huge, but my client became wary when thousands of leads generated almost no business for him. When he sat down to listen to the call recordings, he realized his mistake. Nobody cared about the course - they were only showing up at the trial session to get a free USB stick. The majority of calls were low-quality leads that were actually costing the company money. The radio campaign was worthless.

Fortunately, the company owner was recording his calls. If he had neglected to do so, he'd have no idea why his impressive lead generation was doing nothing for his bottom line. Now, he was able to monitor call quality, geographic area, ad effectiveness, and profitability. We restarted his online campaign, and began the steady climb upwards. Today, his profitability still hasn't plateaued, and we've got the numbers to prove it.

Let's turn back to the case of the dentist's PPC campaign. At the end of the year, she crunches the numbers to see whether her marketing investment makes sense. She simply calculates how much she is spending on PPC, and compares that amount to the revenue generated by PPC prospects. If she's spending $833 each month, any return greater than that justifies the continuation of her marketing campaign.

For our purposes, let's assume that the dentist is generating an additional $1500 per month with her $833 monthly PPC campaign. Seeing that her campaign is working, the dentist decides to increase her marketing budget. She reasons that this winning formula will translate to a bigger return if she puts more money into it. She's not wrong.

However, now it becomes even more important to monitor and measure your results. Remember, many companies have gone down because they ramped up their marketing expenses too quickly. It's like overdriving your headlights - when you speed down the road at night without being able to see what's in front of you, there's a good chance you'll crash.

As a general rule, you should continue to increase your marketing expenses for as long as your campaign continues to be profitable. If the money you invest continues to generate a return greater than the amount you put in, keep raising the bar. Once your profitability stops, your marketing expenses need to be scaled back.

When increasing your marketing expenses, it's best to do so in small increments. This protects you from wastage, optimizes your cost-efficiency, and gives you valuable data that's lost when you ramp up too quickly. If you jump from $833 to $10,000 per month, the numbers will certainly change, but you'll have learned nothing. Not only will you have lost an opportunity for study, but the business you generate will plateau at a certain point. Anything extra you invest will go to waste. meaning you completely wasted the rest of your investment. With small increments, you can consistently creep forward, getting a steady return on your investment, then pump the brakes the second your profitability stops.

Marketing isn't about maybes, guesses, and estimates - it's about securing deals. If you can't link your marketing budget to cold-hard profitability, you're doing it wrong. I'm a numbers guy, and when it comes to marketing, you should be, too. If you can't analyze your data, you can't optimize your advertising.

Assessing Marketing Assets

There's a seemingly infinite number of marketing avenues out there to choose from, but your marketing budget is very finite. How do you choose where to direct your budget?

People always ask me where they should put their money, and I'm always being honest when I tell them that I don't know. Despite my 10 years of experience in advertising, I still have no default answer. Every company has different needs.

I can say that every business should look into online advertising. This is where the majority of your leads will be generated today, no matter what industry you're in. The internet is the lead marketing asset for anything, even life-changing purchases. People now turn the web to find lawyers, book medical procedures, and sign up for their mortgage.

Despite the strength of online marketing, I won't dismiss the value of other assets, and you shouldn't either. Many companies enjoy great success with newspaper ads, radio spots, flyers, cross promotions, and so on.

The best way to find out what works for you is to experiment. If you have the money, I recommend trying a few different options that appeal to you. All you need to do is apply the formula outlined in the previous section. If you put a bit of money into an unsung marketing avenue and see some profitability there, it might be worth pursuing. Just remember to build up in small increments, and scale back once you're no longer generating a positive return.

If you don't have the money to experiment, put your money entirely into online marketing. I really believe that this is the best bang for your buck. Look for a reputable marketing agency, but avoid the "big names" - they will charge you thousands for nothing, matching your budget to cookie-cutter plans. Small, reputable firms with solid reviews are your best bet. Find one where the owners are willing to meet frequently to discuss the results of your campaign.

When you sign on with an online marketing company, you need to make sure your account is being actively managed. Ask questions, request reports, and make an effort to understand what's going on. Clients who don't ask questions often have their accounts abandoned. Marketing firms typically work with dozens of companies at once, and may struggle to maintain their monthly workload as staff resources are stretched thin. If you give them the chance to neglect you without any repercussions, they just might.

Don't try to manage your marketing all by yourself. Beware of anyone telling you that it's easy to figure out on your own. Google AdWords is a simple way to manage your money online, according to Google. The truth is, without a deep knowledge of the industry, you'll end up with suboptimal results, and be taking time away from your real focus: sales, customer care, products, and services. Find a proper company that will manage your account and maximize your budget.

In my experience, finding the best marketers for your company takes time. For 15 years, I sold web projects and mobile applications, and part of the process involved recommending marketing firms to our clients once the work had wrapped up on our end. We didn't have the resources to run multiple online marketing campaigns at the time, so although we had a solid understanding of the industry, we were obligated to point our clients towards the real professionals.

Unfortunately, finding true marketing professionals was easier said than done. We did our best, but many of those we tried working with did not hold themselves to the same standards we did. Most were content to sign up for Google AdWords, throw money at a few keywords, and walk away. Only a special few would take the time to manage your budget and try to improve your campaign performance from month to month.

I kept hearing the same story from different clients; big-name marketers were burning through their budgets with no results or accountability. I heard elaborate pitches from many large companies, but they all boiled down to the same thing: "You put your money down, and we'll do our best."

There are a lot of mediocre companies out there, and you'll need to know how to spot them. After dealing with quite a few, I began to recognize some of the warning signs. They try to dazzle business owners with impressive reports that don't affect their bottom line. As part of their organic SEO strategy, they present the client with a list of keywords to be promoted on a monthly basis, which is standard practice. Soon after, the client starts to see great results on their reports, but no new sales are being generated. How could this be? Does it mean that keyword promotion is a waste of time? Not at all; some marketing companies deliberately try to inflate their reports by targeting non-competitive keywords that do nothing for business. By focusing on unrealistic or impractical search phrases that nobody else is bidding on, the rankings in their reports skyrocket for cheap. Nobody will search using the keywords the marketers bought, but their promotional power looks great on paper because there's no competition. When confronted about their lack of results, the marketing company representative shrugs and says they tried their best. They wash their hands of the client after having bled them for a few months' worth of fees.

Another sign of a bad marketing company is the low-quality traffic scam. Traffic is useless unless it's relevant. If your product is intended for women, advertising to men is a waste of money.

Let's assume that you're paying $500 to bring traffic to your website. The marketers send you a report indicating that your website is getting four times more traffic than it has in the previous month. You're thrilled, until the reality of their service sets in.

You find out that the company has generated irrelevant traffic, using banners, paid sources, and other cheap tricks to drive disinterested users your way. This does nothing for your business; it's as effective as trying to sell a Mercedes to a toddler. The reports look great, but despite the flood of new traffic, your sales rates don't budge. Unsure how they ever ended up on your site, these new visitors leave as quickly as they arrived, driving up your "bounce rate" and causing you to lose precious SEO points. You pay $500, and what do you get? A fancy report and penalties from Google. Your website becomes less visible to searchers, which is the exact opposite of what you hired the company for in the first place.

Finally, keep your eyes out for overpriced paid advertising. I'll use Google Adwords as an example. I am a partner in a web marketing company, and as part of our process, we offer free audits to all prospects. When we take a look at their AdWords accounts, we often find that the client is paying two or three times more than they should. This can be the result of a simple mistake, or something more sinister, but you should keep your guard up either way. We usually find it's a problem with targeting: the account has focused on the wrong demographic or geographic area.

A good company will make an effort to generate quality traffic, manage your paid advertising budget, and present you with a clear and concise monthly report that details expenses versus income. Low-quality companies shy away from this reporting style because it shows their mediocrity. Instead, they'll hand you a stack of papers at the end of the month filled with complicated metrics, then hope that you don't ask too many questions.

Have you ever heard the expression that you should "be the change you want to see"? After 15 years of frustration, I decided to switch my focus from web application development to web marketing so that I could finally get the results I wanted. I partnered with an established marketer with a reputation for "bottom line results, without the B.S." Together, we created 360 Business Local, a boutique marketing company that specializes in conversions, and operates according to the principles outlined in this chapter. Our transparent approach optimizes the online experience from Google search, to landing page arrival, to prospect action, funnelling users through this sales cycle with compelling ads and engaging content. Since the day we opened our doors, we've subjected our process to objective analysis and A/B testing, always striving to find that perfect formula. Most importantly, we involve the client in each and every campaign. We give them precise information about their spending versus sales, and treat them like a partner rather than an ATM. This is the kind of marketing company you need to look for - it won't be easy in a sea of mediocrity, but they're out there!

The Bottom Line

Measurable Marketing

If you can't measure your progress, you'll never reach your goals.

The Entrepreneurial Evolution

Marketing is vital to the success of your business, but avoid blind branding at all costs. Leave branding to the Cokes and Kleenexes of your industry.

All marketing must be treated as a measurable expense. Monitor your data, and continue to increase your marketing budget in small increments for as long as it remains profitable. Once your profitability stops, your marketing budget must be scaled back.

Though online marketing is king, every avenue is worth exploring, as long as you apply the formula outlined in this chapter.

If you don't have the money to spend experimenting, stick to online advertising. But don't do it yourself. Find a small, reputable agency, and stay on top of them to ensure your account is being actively managed.

Try to apply the lessons learned in this chapter to your business. It's time to make some money off of all of your hard work!

Chapter 19: Troubleshooting Sales

Of all the tasks involved in writing this book, trying to summarize my sales approach was probably the most daunting. How could I approach something beyond the scope of fifteen books in a single section?

Anybody who tells you they have the perfect formula for sales is probably lying - if they don't set off your "too good to be true" alarm, I suggest you reread that chapter. The truth is that there's no single formula that applies to every product, industry, and demographic, and if there were one today, it'd be useless in a few months' time. People and markets change rapidly, and sales theory must evolve with them. It's a huge, dynamic subject that cannot be encapsulated in some static curriculum.

I struggled with how to approach this section for some time, but ultimately found an answer by reminding myself of my endgame. I'm not here to teach beginners how to sell; I'm writing this book to increase business owners' profitability, and to help entrepreneurs reach their goals. I don't have to build a comprehensive (and probably impractical) guide - I can go around that impassable obstacle and still achieve my goals.

This chapter is not going to teach you how to conduct sales. If you need to a beginner's guide to sales, you've been reading the wrong book. This lesson is aimed at established business owners who are looking to optimize their existing sales process. Rather than building a sales tutorial from the ground up, I'll share some high-yield troubleshooting tips that address common mistakes and problem areas in the sales process.

The following 7 mini lessons have been designed to make a big impact with little effort. I describe small-scale tweaks and strategic variations that can greatly increase your bottom line. They are all equally important, and often interrelated, so be sure to read them carefully and completely.

The Sales Cycle

Before we go any further, I'd like to review the sales cycle that is referenced throughout this section.

The customer moves through three stages during the sales cycle:

- **Lead** - A lead is a prospective consumer of a product or service. The term is often used to reference someone who has provided contact information that points towards a potential sales opportunity. You could also think of a lead as a person who walks into your store and starts browsing the aisles.
- **Prospect** - A lead become a prospect once they start to interact or negotiate with the salesperson. If your lead approaches the counter with an item in hand and a question in their eyes, they're now a prospect.
- **Client/Customer** - A prospect become a client or a customer once they sign a deal or make a purchase.

Hot and Cold Sales - *"You Can't Cook With Cold Grease"*

When a reporter for the Chicago Tribune asked boxing great Aaron Pryor why he warmed up to disco music before a bout, he famously answered: "You don't cook with cold grease." Pryor didn't know much about business at the time, but he was dropping some unintentional sales knowledge that day.

The majority of your sales will be motivated by emotion. People make most of their purchases in a "hot" frame of mind, whether that means they're fearing deficiencies or excited for results. If they're in a "cold" frame of mind, they're unlikely to buy; you can't cook with cold grease, and you can't sell to cold clients.

So how do you heat the grease? This is where things get tricky. A friend of mine who sells Mercedes is very good at warming cold clients. He treats every interaction like a "hot deal" that needs to be closed as soon as possible, and it does wonders for his bottom line. His closing rate is better than that of his co-workers who use a much more relaxed approach, but I can't say his way is best for everyone.

You can warm up a cold client if you can trigger an emotional response, but there is no universal method. Different prospects will have different needs and emotional triggers, and it takes lots of work, practice, and familiarity with a client to get right. Ask questions, let your prospect speak, and look for pain points; follow the lessons outlined in this chapter, and you'll discover what works best for your unique situation.

It's important that you're able to identify when a client is hot or cold so that you can respond accordingly. If you push hard with someone who has no emotional investment in the product, service, or solution that you're offering, you're just going to turn them off.

There is a right and wrong way to find out whether a prospect is hot or cold, and I'm almost positive you'll have encountered the wrong way by now.

It's very common in North America for business owners to approach a prospect and ask when they intend to purchase the product or service in question. If you enter a Canadian car dealership, you can bet that you'll be asked this question as some point. This is the wrong way to gauge a prospect's temperature.

If you're the salesman asking this question, take their purchase timeline with a grain of salt. This question won't be enough to tell you whether a prospective client is hot or cold.

Granted, if you're dealing with someone representing a large corporate enterprise, things change. Big companies may not have their budget available until a specific quarter, so these clients' timelines will actually mean something.

However, if you're dealing with a smaller company or an individual client, don't put too much stock in their answer. Personal and small-business budgets are not managed as strictly as those belonging to big corporations. These are the "cold" prospects who are worth targeting with your warming efforts. They'll still be willing to buy if you can trigger the right emotion.

Remember that the majority of your sales will be coming from "hot" prospects. Once you stop trying to cook with cold grease, you'll be able to preserve and nurture many more deals. You'll be able to identify which cold clients are worth warming, and which are simply not interested.

Shut Up and Sell

Human beings are driven by ego, and it makes us do stupid, self-destructive things. I've watched ego sabotage business owners' sales more times than I can count, as I wrote in Chapter 8.

I can't tell you how many meetings I've sat in on where a prospect lost interest because the salesperson refused to shut up. They were intoxicated by the attention and authority they commanded as the head speaker. It felt good to keep talking with a room full of people listening, but eventually the prospects got bored. Overindulging the ego in this situation means losing a sale.

I like to remind myself to "shut up and sell." There's a strict limit to how much you should tell a prospect about your product or service. You can't unveil everything all at once, or the appeal will quickly plateau. Once you've filled their cup, any extra information that you add becomes counterproductive. The prospect grows tired of your pitch, and may associate their ennui with your product.

You need to carefully manage how much you fill your prospect's cup during a sales interaction. You can't leave it dry, but you don't want to hit the brim, either; give them a taste of how great your product or service will be, then back off. In true Vegas showman style, you want to leave them wanting more.

Let's assume that you're hosting a sales meeting. You've prepared a top-notch 45-minute presentation.

The meeting is going very well. At the 25-minute mark, your prospects are practically drooling over what you have to offer. They're watching you with wide eyes, and hanging onto your every word.

Do you continue with the final 20 minutes of your presentation? The answer is an emphatic "NO!" A fighter trains for a three-round fight, but he's not going to box two more rounds if he scores a knockout in the first. Your endgame is to sell, not to get an ego boost from an interested audience.

Once you're sure that your prospects are intrigued by your presentation, stop immediately. There is nothing to gain by bombarding them with more information in that moment. You have the prospect in the right frame of mind, so why would you keep trying to sell them on your product or service if they're already sold?

Stop your presentation and ask the prospect how they'd like to proceed or have questions. If they genuinely want to hear more, they'll tell you. If they don't, you'll have saved 20 minutes. More often than not, they'll ask you to continue. Sometimes you'll close the deal on the spot.

Unfortunately, many business owners won't have the discipline needed to end their meeting on a high note. Their egos take over.

If you don't stop the presentation in time, you may stop the sale.

What if the salesmen kept talking in our previous example? 10 minutes later, prospects who were once excited are starting to watch the clock. They're being inundated with information, much of which has nothing to do with what originally attracted them to the offer. The salesperson plows ahead.

By the time the salesperson wraps up, the energy has been completely sucked out of the room. The prospects file out of the meeting like bleary-eyed students after a three-hour lecture, eager to focus on anything other than your spiel.

Make sure you leave your prospects wanting more. There is nothing to gain from continuing a sales presentation to a room full of prospects with nearly-filled cups. Your ego will grow while your bank account shrinks. Offer a few very strong selling points, then assess the client's reaction. Does it make sense to press harder, or is your work here done?

Remember that your endgame is to make a sale, not to stroke your ego or practice your public speaking. Assess the situation as an objective observer, rather than someone with their ego invested, then move forward with whatever action is needed to secure the sale. Do only what is necessary.

Premade Pitches

As I wrote in the introduction, there are no one-size-fits-all sales solutions. Premade pitches don't work; people are vastly different from one another, with very different needs. If you want to increase your closing rate, discard the cookie-cutter sales pitch.

A prospect's interest in your product or service is usually based on a specific need, whether it helps them solve a problem they're having, or improves some aspect of their life.

The conversation that you have during the sales cycle will usually involve many questions related to your these needs. If I'm buying a car, I may ask questions about gas mileage, safety ratings, or hauling power. I'll be attracted to different features depending on how I intend to use my new vehicle.

This is where premade sales pitches start to crumble apart. Even the most thorough premade sales pitch will probably only cover a few of items that I want to discuss. Why would I care to hear about the car's safety rating and hauling power when all I want is good gas mileage? Talking about these features is a complete waste of my time. I'd rather use that time to hear about other cars that are good on gas. You may pique my interest by mentioning gas efficiency early on, then lose me as your presentation continues, as discussed in the previous lesson.

You don't make business by describing every detail of your product or service - you make business by presenting your offering as something that meets the client's needs. This can only be done if you toss out the premade pitch.

Ask questions of your own, and listen to what your client has to say. When you let your client talk, you achieve two important things. First, you get more face time. The more time you spend talking to the client, the greater the chances that they'll start to see you as a friend, rather than a sales-pitching automaton. This will make them more willing to listen, trust, and buy.

Secondly, asking questions gives you vital information that can be used to create a conversation based on their specific needs. The prospect will tell you their "pain points," which you can use to increase the value of your offer. Assess what it is your prospect needs, then custom-build the interaction to present your product or service as the solution. If I keep asking about gas mileage, it's safe to assume that's what I'm interested in, and your focus should shift accordingly.

Remember that your endgame is to sell, not to share all of your knowledge about a particular product or service. If you have to withhold some of your hard-earned information for the sake of a sale, then so be it!

Know-It-All Syndrome

"Know-It-All Syndrome" is a sales-killing disease that runs rampant in the business world. In fact, we all carry the "Know-It-All" strain - some of us are just able to keep it dormant.

The problem arises when the salesperson knows better than their prospect, which is almost always going to be the case. If you're a true professional who knows your product or service inside-out, there's very little little chance that you'll ever meet a prospect who knows more than you. This is the way it should be.

Though you should "know it all," you can't come across as a Know-It-All. Knowledge is power, and it must be wielded carefully; the second you make your prospect feel small or unknowledgeable, you will lose the sale.

In 2014, I ordered a VoIP phone system for one of my offices. I encountered a salesperson with a bad case of Know-It-All syndrome. I'm no expert in VoIP, but I had some idea of what I wanted and how I intended to implement it. The salesperson wasn't hearing it. He shot my idea down straight away, then launched into a series of diagrams and mock-ups that showed what he insisted was the "right way."

This salesperson was extremely lucky not to lose a prospect that day. I have worked long and hard to detach my ego from my business dealings. I try to remain open to all new knowledge, and don't take it personally when someone flexes their expertise. I know that I'm no expert in VoIP, so I chose to listen, though I'll admit his dismissal of my ideas still stung. I was probably his first sale in some time.

For the majority of people, the Know-It-All approach is a huge turn off. Remember that human beings are driven by ego. If you tell somebody who carries their ego to work that they're "absolutely wrong" during a sales meeting, you might as well pack up and go, because the deal is dead. Your sales cycle must be "politically correct," and you must remain diplomatic while telling someone that they're wrong.

If a prospect has the wrong information, you have to work with it, not reject it. Even if a client is 100% mistaken, you have to acknowledge that their idea is valid, then present your method as another option. Take what they give you, twist it in a positive light, and offer a reasonable alternative. Even if the prospect proposes the dumbest idea you've ever heard, they should walk out of that meeting feeling like they contributed to the discussion.

When offering your alternative, the key is to present your idea as something that most people don't know about. "That's a good idea, but there's another option that many people are unfamiliar with. Allow me to explain." By framing your solution in this way, you avoid offending or embarrassing the prospect. They feel like they're being let in on a new, uncommon piece of information, rather than feeling stupid for not knowing something obvious.

Do everything you can to fight off the Know-It-All Syndrome, or it will take you down. It doesn't matter how much your product or service stands to help a prospect; the sting of a burned ego will overshadow any value you're offering, and they'll walk away from the meeting with negative feelings about you.

Offer A Look Beyond the Sales Cycle

While taking a prospective client through the sales cycle, it's imperative that you explain in vivid detail what the "next steps" will be. Prospective clients will take great comfort in knowing what comes after their purchase. This kind of transparency is what separates the amateurs from the professionals.

Giving clients a look beyond the sales cycle has helped me succeed in highly competitive industries. Operating in an oversaturated web design market, I was able to land project after project without issue. Friends and colleagues were shocked; there was a huge inventory of web design companies to choose from, many with monstrous marketing budgets, but my small company's sales remained strong and steady.

How was I able to stay afloat in a highly competitive industry? What attracted so many clients to my process?

The main difference between me and my competitors was that I laid my process out in detail for the client to see. While working with other firms, my clients had been left in the dark, forced to wait and hope things were going well behind the scenes after their order had been processed. This guessing game was a huge turn off.

In contrast, I would tell them everything they wanted. I'd explain that the first step was to locate a development server where their website can be built, and that they'd be given full access to their project at every stage. I'd outline a system of milestones to keep them updated about exactly when and how their project was progressing, then establish two meeting times each week where we could respond to any feedback or questions they might have. My goal was to make the client feel like a partner for the duration of their project.

When you lay your process out in this way, the client sees that you're a professional. They will appreciate this information, and realize that you're not trying to rip them off. You become an authority in their eyes. Even if they decide to go with another company, they'll be comparing their new provider's plan with the one you delivered, and will come back to you if it's found wanting. You'll be surprised at how often this happens; a startling amount of businesses are run by amateurs who leave their clients completely in the dark.

Of course, this lesson must synergize with the previous ones. Your plan should be custom-built around the needs that the customer expressed during your interaction, and you'll need to be mindful of your ego as you deliver it. Don't overfill their cup with details.

Expose the Scam

Every industry has scams. I guarantee that you've been targeted for one at some point in your life, though the chances are dropping as time goes on.

10-15 years ago, an unscrupulous salesperson could get away with some seriously shady practices, but not today. In the past, only the industry insiders knew how to the game worked, but these days are done. The internet has given power to the people; forums, review websites, online tutorials, and the general ease of access to information has make it very hard for "industry secrets" to persist. People know everything nowadays, and they're on the lookout for scams.

The internet era is one of transparency and accountability, and you need to embrace this mentality. If you do, you'll earn your prospect's trust, and put yourself in a much stronger position to sell. This book is intended for people who want to come by sales honestly, but if you're still not convinced that you should leave your industry "tricks" behind, this section should help.

Troubleshooting Sales

" You know what? I like you. I'm going to throw in the rust proofing for free."

Biplov '16

The Entrepreneurial Evolution

Imagine that you're a car salesperson who has decided to take my advice. Your industry is rife with scams, and, if you're trying to close deals, exposing them should be your first priority. Take your time to explain what differentiates you from the scam-artists that populate your industry, and you'll see results.

First, you tell your prospect about the "test drive" trick. "Other salespeople are going to offer to join you for a test drive. They'll use the ride to leech as much information from you as possible, and start pressuring you to buy right away."

Next, you explain the "manager discount game" that your competitors play. "When you arrive back at the dealership, they'll make a real show of trying to get you a discount. They'll march into the back room, where a pantomime showdown with their manager will be on full display through the office door. They'll walk out looking triumphant, and quietly describe the 'amazing deal' you just got, whispering as if the other customers are going to get jealous."

Finally, you unveil the "upsell scam." "When you're reading to sign on, they'll hit you with hidden costs and upgraded feature fees. When you're exhausted and ready to sign whatever you're given, they'll close the sale at the price they had intended to give you in the first place."

Now you can give your honest, transparent alternative. "I'll give you the best price I can upfront, and I'll let you test drive the car on your own so you can have fun with it. If everything looks and feels the way you want it, I'll be happy to help. No pressure."

Once you've laid the industry scam out for the prospect, you'll gain their trust. It will help your closing rate a lot. There's a good chance that the person in front of you already knows about the scam you're describing, so you'll gain a lot of respect by being forthright. The prospect knows that you won't try to scam them using the process you just described, and they'll acknowledge your authority on the subject since you're echoing the "insider information" they already read online. If they entered the interaction feeling hesitant or guarded, they'll quickly "warm up." They'll be open to feelings of excitement and interest in your product or service. Once you've exposed the scam, you can turn a cold prospect into a hot one in no time. They'll be much more open to the idea of doing business with you. And because you were honest, you'll both be able to walk away from the interaction with a good feeling.

Every industry has a scam - some have many. Try this method, and you'll separate yourself from the scammers that keep clients on guard.

Homerun Hunting

Every entrepreneur wants to close big deals, and there's nothing wrong with that. However, if you're hunting for home runs with every swing, you're going to strike out more often.

I saw a classic case of homerun hunting while sitting in on a recent meeting hosted by a salesperson in training. I was there as an observer and consultant, and had arranged the meeting through a friend of mine. The deal was ours to lose.

The prospects told the salesperson that they were having problems with their metrics. They weren't happy with their current analysis of how leads become sales. They wanted specific help with their conversion process, and were very interested in what our company had to offer in this area.

Rather than focusing on their conversion process, the salesperson in training continued describing some of the other services that our company offered. I noticed our prospects stealing glances at their watches and leaning subconsciously towards the doorway. Their body language indicated that they'd heard enough.

Fortunately, someone in the room asked another question about the conversion process, ignoring the salesperson's pitch about unrelated services. I thought we had a chance. The salesperson explained our metric analysis package in greater detail, regaining everyone's attention for a brief moment.

Unfortunately, he couldn't help himself. Less than two minutes later, he was chasing that home run again, explaining our full suite of services. The prospects had finally had enough and announced that we had to wrap up, as they were short on time. They dismissed us, and off we went.

Where did the salesperson in training go wrong? Almost every lesson in this section applies. He certainly didn't "shut up and sell." Our prospects hardly had a chance to speak, and their questions were unaddressed by what appeared to be a "premade pitch." He wasn't asking questions or exploring their needs. He wasn't giving them a glimpse beyond the sales cycle, choosing to explain unrelated services rather than shining light on our metric analysis plan. I had set him up for success, and it had all gone wrong.

When I spoke to the salesperson in training, he couldn't see his mistakes. I told him that he hadn't followed my advice, but he seemed unphased. He believed he had made the right choice. After all, the metric services we offered only generate about $1,000 monthly. The salesperson in training was hunting our $60,000 service package instead.

This kind of home run hunting is obviously a huge mistake. We had an opportunity to take $1,000 per month, and build a strong connection with a valuable client. Once the relationship had been secured and trust had been built, we could have started probing for the bigger packages. We could have become their main vendor, so long as we did a good job with the metric analysis (which we certainly would have). The salesperson in training decided to throw it all away to chase a home run. Instead of a promising client relationship and $12,000 per year, we were left with nothing.

Don't get caught up hunting for home runs.

Continue Your Evolution

I've made my online course available to all readers. It's complete with video lectures, homework assignments, and chapter quizzes. You can see the course curriculum in its entirety at http://employer.rapidbusinesslessons.com/. Click "Get Started" and enter coupon code "employer-dream" to redeem your free membership. You'll also be given access to unlimited copies of our freelancer course, which is meant to be distributed to all outsourcing hires to ensure everyone is working from the same playbook.

I created RapidBusinessLessons.com for the same reasons I wrote this book. However, the online medium has certain advantages. Video and audio components make for a more engaging learning experience, and you can update a website as often as you want. If you enjoyed what you read here, I encourage you to explore our growing archive of online courses for business owners. Check back regularly, or register for automatic updates; there are currently 10 courses slated for release in 2016, and more on the way as business educators continue to sign on to share new methods.

I hope you've enjoyed *The Entrepreneurial Evolution*. The method I've shared here is highly effective, but it's not the be all and end all; remember, static textbook curriculums don't work for long in the business world. Your evolution must be dynamic, part of a feedback loop whose outcome is never final. This book is just another step forward.

Your development as an entrepreneur will be unique. It's a highly personal journey without a predictable arc. You'll experience ups, and what feel like downs; but with the right mindset, you'll always be evolving. Try to learn as much as possible from every interaction, and build positive experiences everywhere you can. Put your ego aside and drill your fundamentals. Keep your eyes open for growth opportunities.

Good luck out there!

About the Author

Lior Izik is a hacker, hunter, martial artist, and family man, but above all, an entrepreneur. Since 1995, Mr. Izik has founded, managed, and developed numerous companies into successful entities. His portfolio includes projects with industry leaders like Johnson & Johnson, Siemens, T Mobile, Revlon, JVC, CDS, Otsuka and Osler, as well as ongoing consultative work with small business owners around the world.

Mr. Izik has been an active and cutting-edge contributor to the business world for many years. His vision for better business has inspired the release of a number of online courses. Become a Successful Freelancer – Step By Step is currently available on Amazon in 9 different languages, and its companion course is slated to release in early 2016, along with anti-bullying project and application security curricula at https://www.rapidbusinesslessons.com/.

www.ingramcontent.com/pod-product-compliance
Lightning Source LLC
Chambersburg PA
CBHW070240190526
45169CB00001B/250

* 9 7 8 1 5 3 4 6 6 4 5 9 3 *